DRAMA IN THE CHURCH

DRAMA IN THE CHURCH
A Manual of Religious Drama Production

BY

FRED EASTMAN

AND

LOUIS WILSON

SAMUEL FRENCH

Founded 1830   Incorporated 1899

25 WEST 45TH ST.   NEW YORK

811 WEST 7TH ST.   LOS ANGELES

MANUFACTURED IN THE UNITED STATES OF AMERICA
BY THE VAIL-BALLOU PRESS, INC., BINGHAMTON, N. Y.

AT one of our early Christmas celebrations Longfellow's *Golden Legend* was given, the actors portraying it with the touch of the miracle play spirit which it reflects. I remember an old blind man, who took the part of a shepherd, said, at the end of the last performance, "Kind Heart," a name by which he always addressed me, "it seems to me that I have been waiting all my life to hear some of these things said. I am glad we had so many performances, for I think I can remember them to the end. It is getting hard for me to listen to reading, but the different voices and all made this very plain." Had he not perhaps made a legitimate demand upon the drama, that it shall express for us that which we have not been able to formulate for ourselves, that it shall warm us with a sense of companionship with the experiences of others; does not every genuine drama present our relations to each other and to the world in which we find ourselves in such wise as may fortify us to the end of the journey?

—From Jane Addams' *Twenty Years at Hull House.*

FOREWORD

A FRIEND came into my study the other day as the manuscript of the following chapters lay on my desk. He asked what it was all about. I told him that it was a manual of religious drama production. Thereupon this conversation took place:

He: What do you mean—"religious drama"? Methodist? Presbyterian? Baptist? Congregationalist?

I: Of course not. I said, "religious," not sectarian.

He: Protestant? Roman Catholic? Jewish?

I: Religious drama includes them all.

He: Then you mean biblical drama?

I· I don't. There are many religious plays which are not biblical.

He: Oh, now I understand. You mean propaganda plays.

I (tearing my hair): Heaven forbid!

He: Well, then, I give up. What *do* you mean?

I: Simply this: a religious drama is one that has a religious effect upon a congregation.

He: But when does a play have a religious effect?

I: When it sends the congregation away exalted in spirit and with a deeper sense of fellowship with God and man.

He: I've had some such experience occasionally in watching a play in a theatre.

I: Good! I was beginning to wonder—

He: We'll let that pass for the moment. What I
want to know is: have you explained that definition to your prospective readers?

I: We've mentioned it somewhere—but mostly we
have assumed it.

He: You'd better write it at the beginning—and
write it large—for everybody has his own idea
of religious drama and you can't be sure it's the
same as yours.

He was right, of course. So we are putting it here,
that the reader may know from the start what we mean
by the term religious drama.

Another thing should be made plain before going
further: We have not written one more manual of amateur drama production. Instead, we have tried to create
a practical manual that sums up in brief compass the
most important things drama groups should know for
the task of *producing plays in churches—not as entertainment but as a means of ministering to the souls of
men through a great art.*

With this specific purpose in mind we have tried to
condense what we have learned—or think we have
learned—from three sources. First, from many years
of experience in producing religious dramas—hundreds
of them—in everything from a remote rural church to
a great university chapel. Second, from the players and
the back-stage crews. After each play every member of
the cast and of the back-stage crew has been asked to
write a brief paper on what he learned from the experience. These human documents have been accumulat-
ing until they have crowded our files and demanded a
chance to tell their story to other players and other
crews. Third, from the study of the books written by
those who have been doing similar work in the field of

drama generally. Among these the most comprehensive and significant are Alexander Dean's *Fundamentals of Play Directing*, William Kozlenko's *The One-Act Play*, Hume and Foster's *Theater and School*, John Dolman Jr.'s *The Art of Play Production*, and Mordecai Gorelik's *New Theatres for Old*. We acknowledge gratefully our indebtedness to these.

We hope that this condensation may be of some use to the ever increasing number of churches which are finding in the drama a means of developing beauty and power in the spiritual life of players and of audiences.

Parts of this manual have appeared separately in print —the Introduction in *The Christian Century*, "Historical Background" in a pamphlet published by the Century Company of New York, and "Equipment" in *Church Management*. We wish to thank the editors for their permission to include these articles here.

F. E.

CONTENTS

DRAMA IN THE CHURCH

Introduction

HOW TO KILL RELIGIOUS DRAMA

Wish it upon the children. They did very well dramatizing a Bible story in a classroom, so of course they will know how to produce an adult drama before an audience. They may learn something from it and it can't do them any harm. If they make such a mess of it that no one but their parents and aunts will come to their future productions, what of it? By then some newer wrinkle may come along to intrigue children's fancies.

Turn it over to the choir director. He's a good fellow and will know how to handle the music. He likes to go to the movies and must have picked up a lot of dramatic technique there. He has an eye for color and will know what to do about costumes. Besides, he's at the church two or three times during the week for choir rehearsal and might just as well stay a little longer and direct a religious drama. To be sure, he doesn't know anything about the Bible or the art of play production, but whatever he produces will have good music and make pretty pictures on the platform, so what's the difference?

If the choir director won't take charge of it, give it over to some nice young girl who once had a part in a high school play. She ought to know what's what. And the young people like her. Don't bother them with manuals of play production by more experienced persons. It will be sort of democratic to let them work things out together.

Choose only non-royalty plays. These will cut down the expense. Why waste five dollars or ten on a drama when one just as long and involving even more characters can be secured for only thirty cents a copy from denominational headquarters? What if the cheaper play lacks dramatic power and is loaded to the muzzle with propaganda? It is clean and harmless. And its message ties in with the every member canvass. If the congregation tires of the propaganda plays, why, the play publishers have long lists of plays that require no royalty whatever. Anyway, no one should expect too much of a play in a church.

Provide no equipment for it. Instead, inspire the group to "demonstrate what can be done under a handicap." Avoid any platform or stage larger than is necessary for a pulpit. Don't waste money on lighting. Borrow properties from the minister's house. A few yards of cheese-cloth or cambric strung upon a sagging wire will do for a curtain. If the curtain sticks at the critical moment—well, don't all amateur curtains stick? Won't the audience overlook such deficiencies if the director will just come out and offer a smiling apology and ask the congregation to "let its imagination supply these items"?

Follow the play with a sermon pointing out the moral and urging greater gifts to the church.

Drama is a tough old art and religious drama is as ancient as recorded history, but any of the above prescriptions will knock it out. Two or three in combination will prove fatal within a year.

RELIGIOUS DRAMA'S RIGHT TO EXIST

These melancholy reflections arise from contemplation of the data turned up by a study recently completed

by the religious drama department of the Chicago Theological Seminary. The study sought to discover the
extent and nature of the use of religious drama in the
Midwest. Three hundred and sixty-four churches supplied the information. Not all of it was depressing, and
we shall come to the brighter side soon. But we may
well pause for a moment to recall some words of the
late Professor Gerald Birney Smith:

A new tendency in church idealism is making itself felt
with astonishing rapidity. Protestantism has suddenly become
conscious of the inartistic quality of many phases of its portrayal of religion. The ugliness of many church buildings,
the all-too-prevalent lack of dignity in the conduct of worship, the dreadful quality of the music in many churches
—these have all suddenly flashed upon our vision as im-
pediments to profound religious experience. We are on the
threshold of a strong desire to improve the aesthetic quality
of Protestantism.

It is only as the aesthetic side of Protestantism shall be
taken as seriously as its intellectual and pedagogical aspects
that we shall be able in the perplexing age before us to commend our faith with all the power and dignity which it
deserves. If Protestantism is worth preserving it can be pre-
served only as it shall be made as obviously dignified and
worthy as Catholicism. But this dignifying of Protestantism
cannot be a mere imitation; it must develop its own original
worship and its own original aesthetic forms.

Note again that clause: "to commend our faith with
all the power and dignity which it deserves." Therein
lies the answer to churches which have been committing
drama to the children and without adequate direction,
good plays, or suitable equipment. Such treatment of a
great art will never enable it to commend our faith with
either dignity or power.

In drama religion has an ally whose potential ability to develop beauty and strength in the spiritual life is comparable only to that of music. In some respects it is even greater than music, for the drama, more than music, has to do with the revelation of human character. Any church that chooses cheap hymnals, hires a poor organist, installs a flimsy organ and a gum-chewing choir, kills music; and it kills also something fine and sensitive in the spiritual life of its congregation. Just so for drama. It is a great art and must be taken seriously if it is to yield its blessings. It will not yield them through cheap, inartistic, and propaganda plays.

EXTENT OF ITS USE [1]

Now for the rest of the study—and its brighter side. Of the 364 churches studied in sixteen states of the middle west, 322 reported that they had produced a total of 947 plays during the year. That is an average of 2.9 plays per church.

For purposes of the survey a religious drama was defined as "one which has a religious effect upon an audience; that is, it sends the audience away exalted in spirit and with a deeper sense of fellowship with God and man." Religious dramas were further considered of two kinds: biblical and non-biblical. A third category called non-religious dramas was added so that the classification could be complete. Of the 947 plays produced the churches reporting them classified 318 as "biblical," 425 as "non-biblical but religious," and 125 as "non-religious." The remaining 79 were not classified.

In answer to the question, "For what purpose does

[1] The statistics in this section are taken from a master of arts thesis entitled "A Study of Religious Drama in Certain Churches of Six Protestant Denominations in the United States" by Jean Starr Williams, The Chicago Theological Seminary, 1941.

the church produce dramas?" 290 replies checked the words, "For the inspiration of the audience"; 110 checked the words, "For the education of the players"; 66 checked the words, "To raise money"; while 24 checked, "For entertainment and other purposes."

When were the plays given? Most of them were presented at the Sunday evening worship service; some at the young people's meeting, and a few at the meetings of the Ladies' Aid, men's club, and other gatherings. Among the special days on the church calendar, Christmas drew the largest percentage, Easter next, and Children's Day, third. But only 40 per cent of all the plays were produced on special occasions; the rest in connection with regular services of the church.

Apparently most of this dramatic production has been done without special equipment, for only 30 per cent of the churches reported that they had permanent stage, curtains, and lights, and only 18 per cent more reported that they had these as temporary facilities.

So much for the bare facts. These figures reveal that the churches are using drama rather extensively. Much of this drama is of poor quality, without adequate equipment or direction. But the churches would not be using drama at all unless they found value in it. And if they have found value in the type of drama that most of them produce, how much more value will they find when they take it as seriously as the most effective churches have learned to take their music!

RAISING THE STANDARDS

Some churches do take it so. There is a heartening minority whose lists of plays show discrimination, and whose direction has been disciplined by careful study.

There are still more which have recently added worthy equipment. Several report that they have established religious drama tournaments, interdenominational and community-wide, in order to raise the standards and demonstrate the value of good drama in the educational and worship services of the church. More than three hundred of the churches requested a selected list of better plays. And compared with a similar study made in 1931 there has been no little advance.

The tendency is toward modern plays of spiritual power rather than biblical plays; and toward production for the inspiration of the audience in the Sunday evening worship service rather than for revenue on week nights.

WHAT DRAMA CAN CONTRIBUTE

Two examples will illustrate what drama can contribute to the culture of the human spirit. The first is from ancient Greece. For nearly five hundred years the Athenians made drama their chief means of adult religious education. They housed it in their most sacred temple. They presented their greatest dramas there at the sacred season of the year. They closed their places of business, adjourned their courts, and even opened their jails so that everyone might come and receive the intellectual and spiritual stimulus of the plays. So powerful was the effect of those religious dramas that Athenians developed an understanding and an insight which made their name a symbol of culture from that day to this. Read those plays today—the dramas of Aeschylus, Sophocles, and Euripides especially—and you will see why they have lived for twenty-four hundred years. There is life in them, and a striving after truth, and there is supreme beauty.

Another example is that of the Canterbury cathedral. Several years ago it decided to produce a religious drama at Christmas time. It considered the possible playwrights, selected England's leading poet, John Masefield, and asked him to write a poetic drama, "The Coming of Christ." Next it asked Gustav Holst, a foremost composer, to create the music. Then it secured the best available players, singers, and director. The result was a play of power and beauty that will probably live as long as the English language lives. *That* is taking drama seriously.

How can modern American churches achieve through religious drama results comparable to those of the Greeks or of Canterbury cathedral? By treating it with the same respect. By cultivating it in our temples. By giving it the best equipment, not the worst. By encouraging our best dramatists and players to consecrate at least a part of their talents to Christian service. By putting our younger players and playwrights through a rigorous discipline. By choosing the best plays, not the cheapest. By entrusting drama, not to the immature, but to those whose own struggles have brought to them that refinement of spirit essential to a sympathetic portrayal of human character in action.

Chapter I

THE HISTORICAL BACKGROUND

THOSE who produce religious drama may take more joy in their work and do a better job at it if they know something of its historical background. It is a long, long background, bloody in spots, and across it the peoples of the earth have marched. For the history of every civilization reveals that its drama has grown out of its early religious ceremonies. Having grown out of them, however, it has not always remained friendly and the mother religion has frequently come to regard her drama child as a prodigal son. To show how religion and drama at their best have helped each other when they have worked together and suffered when they have worked against each other, and how they may be of mutual assistance in the crisis which each faces today—such is our purpose in this chapter.

RELIGION AND DRAMA IN ANCIENT GREECE

The story can be told by a series of snap-shots. The first is in an ancient Greek temple, the temple of Dionysus, in the fifth century before Christ. Picture an audience of 20,000 Athenians and others sitting for six days in the great amphitheatre of that temple witnessing the production of twenty-five or thirty plays—and you picture the greatest experiment in adult religious education which the world has ever seen. Those plays were no commercial project of the Greeks, nor were they aesthetic only. To the Greeks they were the principal means of cultivating the spiritual and ethical life. The state sponsored the dramatic contests and regarded them as so important that during the productions all business was abandoned, the law courts closed, and prisoners were even released from jail that they might profit by the spiritual stimulus of the plays. The poets who wrote those plays, the actors who played them, and the coregi who paid the cost of production were all looked upon as ministers of religion and their persons held sacred and inviolable. The amphitheatre itself possessed the sanctity of a temple. Anyone who committed a misdemeanor in the temple during a play made himself liable not merely to the usual penalty for such an act, but to the penalty of death as having committed a sacrilege. These plays had developed gradually out of the songs and dances in honor of Dionysus, the god of wine and vegetation. In the course of time they developed into something far more important than an act of homage to a god, but they did not lose their essentially religious character and they continued to be acted in the temple, and at the season of the year regarded as most sacred. The interest of the people was so keen that more than half the entire population of Athens turned out to see the plays. And so successful did the state count the project that it maintained it for nearly five hundred years—until the Roman conquest of Greece. Here is our first example of religion and drama working together.

DECLINE UNDER ROME

Now let us look at another picture of what happened to the drama when it was separated from religion. Imagine a Roman theatre of the second century. Rome has conquered Greece and has taken over Greek drama—but Rome is not interested in a drama which portrays the struggles of the soul or seeks to interpret the mysteries of life. She is interested only in a theatre that provides an *escape* from life—something that will entertain, arouse passions, provide thrills. And so the drama under Roman influence has become a bloody and obscene spectacle. Again you have thousands in an amphitheatre— but they have not come to worship or to think. They have come to see gladiators fight, and wild animals turned loose upon helpless prisoners, and Christian martyrs burned as torches around the theatre. Three thousand Christians burned in a Roman theatre in a single day! The Christians didn't care for this sort of drama and so, when the Christian religion came into power in Rome, one of its first official acts was to put its foot upon the theatre and crush it. And that is a picture of what happened when religion and drama worked against each other.

REBIRTH OF DRAMA IN THE CHURCH OF THE MIDDLE AGES

Let the centuries roll by and take another snap-shot in England of the Middle Ages. The Drama has had a re-birth in England, and it has been cradled in the church. The language of the church is Latin and the common people have not understood it. The priests wishing to make the gospel story clear have dramatized it. They have introduced passion plays dealing with the life of Christ and acted them in the chancel. The people have understood and asked for more. Saints' plays acted in the nave have followed. Then came mystery plays. Our next picture shows an out-door stage at the entrance of the church, a huge crowd gathered around it. That crowd watches in reverence while a whole cycle of plays, anywhere from fifteen to fifty, are presented in sequence. They are all episodes in one great story—the story of God's relation to the human race as told in the Bible from Genesis to Revelation, from the Creation to Judgment Day. Guilds of laymen are doing the acting and they have felt free to interpret the Bible stories with much imaginative material of their own mixed in. For example, in the episode dealing with the Flood we recognize Noah driving the animals into the ark. That has a biblical air about it—but after the animals are in he has much greater difficulty in persuading his wife to come along. And when he finally gets her aboard he is so weary with the job that he comes forward and urges the young men in the audience to be warned and take their wives in hand early in life and "chastise thare tong." Mrs. Noah thereupon comes forward and warns the ladies that if they are wise they will never marry at all. Now this seems to have been left out of the Bible which we know. Nevertheless it represents an interpretation of a Bible story in terms of the experience of medieval England, and the people understand it and like it and want more.

Look at a typical stage on which these old dramas were presented. A curious affair—plain wooden platform with two stories, one for dressing room, the other for action. At one end are the pearly gates of heaven, at the other the flaming jaws of Hell-mouth. At the end of the play all the good characters go into the pearly gates of heaven, and all the bad characters into the jaws

of hell.[1] Very simple, isn't it? But for all its crudity and
naïveté it is rather an effective attempt of religion and
drama to work together to make life more interesting
and abundant.

ANOTHER DECLINE

Our next snap-shot is taken in the year 1643. It is of
men going about the city of London and tacking upon
the doors of every theatre a notice to the effect that the
theatre is now closed by ordinance of the Lords and
Commons because the public stage has become "sub-
versive of public morals." One of the excesses of Puri-
tanism? Yes, in part, it is the result of a religion that has
gone sour. But not entirely. The stage has been going to
excesses in the other direction. It has made sport of
sacred things. It has been irreverent and obscene. It has
scoffed at decency and integrity. All in all our picture is
one of a time when religion and drama are working
against each other.

How did it come to pass that religion and drama which
were helping one another so happily in the 14th century
should be quarreling so bitterly in the 17th? The answer
is complicated, of course, but one old legend throws a bit
of light upon it. According to this legend *Punch and
Judy* is a contraction of Pontius Pilate and Judas Iscariot.
And this is the way the contraction came about: Pontius
Pilate and Judas Iscariot were two great tragic personalities which appeared in all the old mystery cycles when
they were presented on that queer stage in the entrances
of the churches. But in time someone thought of putting

---

[1] The bad characters wore costumes of black and orange, which,
according to Prof. Adams of Yale, inspired a student to write, in an
examination paper, "the damned souls who went to hell all wore the
Princeton colors."

that stage on wheels and rolling it out to other parts of the city and even into the provinces. That made the first pageant—for the word pageant means "rolling platform." Now when the plays were taken out over the city on these rolling platforms they drew crowds. The innkeepers saw these crowds and realized that here was a chance for business. So it is not difficult to imagine them appealing to the actors and saying in substance, "Here, if you will come and present your plays in the courtyard of the inn we will see that you have food and drink and lodging." The players were human and consented. So in time the plays were presented in the courtyards of the inns instead of at the churches. But the audiences were different. The audiences about the church had come in a spirit of reverence and worship. The audiences about the inn had come for amusement and hilarity. These audiences around the inns were a great deal more interested in the characters who went into the flaming jaws of hell at the end of the play than in those who went into the pearly gates of heaven. The players in those days had a great deal more to do with their lines than they have since. They began to change their lines and their interpretation of character to meet the demands of these inn audiences for more laughter and more fun. And so in the course of a century or more these great tragic characters Pontius Pilate and Judas Iscariot had introduced buffoonery into their parts, making them comic rather than tragic. And then in the course of further years they became mere puppets—Punch and Judy.

This legend is probably not historical. But it is as true to the inner sequence of events in the theatre as though it were. For this is certain: the drama of medieval England lost its sense of being a mirror of the soul, it became a show business, and then, in spite of the tremendous influence of Marlowe and Shakespeare to the contrary, a thing of questionable value and decency. Religion lost its appreciation of the dramatic struggles of human life, became dogmatic and other-worldly, and went around not only kicking wickedness out of high places, but also kicking beauty out of the churches and pleasure out of human life.

THE PRESENT CRISIS IN RELIGION AND DRAMA

Enough of these snap-shots of history. Here we are in the twentieth century. We need no pictures now for we can use our own eyes. And what do we see? Religion at a crisis. Drama at a crisis. Churches bemoaning the decline of their authority; theatres struggling for existence and wondering what sort of show-business to tackle next to make money and make it quick. History is repeating itself before our eyes. *The question is, which history shall it be—the history of religion and drama working together or religion and drama working against each other? That question is for us to answer. And a good bit of the spiritual history of this century will be determined by the answer we give during the next few years.*

Let us look at the situation in our churches and our theatres a little more closely. Let us see what forces are operating to make religion and drama work together for the benefit of mankind, and what forces are operating to drive them apart and to work against each other.

There is a bloody battle going on between a group of men who control large areas of the theatre and are interested in drama for revenue only and another smaller group who look upon drama as an art whose duty and privilege it is to mirror the struggles of human souls. The first group are the spiritual descendants of the old inn-keeper crowd of the Middle Ages. The second group are the spiritual children of the old Greek poets. The first group care only for shows that will make quick money and these are usually shows that provide an escape from life. The second group, like true artists, care for drama which provides *not an escape, but an interpretation* of life. The inn-keeper crowd give us crook plays, obscene plays, and musical comedies of a frothy sort. The artist crowd give us the plays of Shaw, Galsworthy, Anderson, O'Neill, Barry, Green, and Wilder. Between the inn-keeper crowd and the artists the battle is joined. The issue of that battle is the life or death of the drama as an art. The victory will go in the long run as we and our fellow citizens vote at the box offices.

If the artists' battle against the inn-keepers were entirely confined to the regular theatres we might feel pessimistic over the prospect. But it is not. Many of them in America and England have set up Little Theatres half-professional and half-amateur. It is a rare city in America which does not have its little theatre today. It may be housed in a stable or an old saloon, a box-car or an abandoned grocery store. It may have only cheese-cloth for curtains and more cheese-cloth for costumes. Its lighting may consist of only half a dozen smoky lanterns of which someone said that if we had a few more of them we would have absolute darkness. Its treasury may be microscopic. But for all that it has youth and enthusiasm and vision. It is producing the classics and new plays with thumb tacks and gusto. Mr. Kenneth Macgowan in his book, *Footlights Across America,* estimates that there are "at least 1000 groups that give one or two plays each season, 6000 high schools that produce as part of their class work anywhere from one bill of short plays to 25 bills of long and short, and 6000 more high schools with dramatic clubs that give at least one play a year." This movement has already given to the world such artists as Stanislawski, Reinhardt, Synge, and Brieux in Europe, and O'Neill and Paul Green in America. It has also given us the Theatre Guild and the Group Theatre and various Civic repertory theatres. Any movement that can bear such fruit must have the divine spark in it. The inn-keeper crowd may kill the regular theatres for us— but these young people will raise it from the dead.

And now let us turn to the present situation in religion, mindful that our view must not be limited to any one sect or denomination. In every division of Christianity and Judaism today, there are two main groups, one looking upon religion as a means of escape from the miseries of human life, and the other looking upon religion as a source of power to help us understand these miseries, to battle with them, and transform them. It is not in our province here to weigh one philosophy against the other. But when we come to consider these groups with relation to drama we find a distinct difference. The first group, which is and always has been by far the larger, takes little interest in drama except in certain forms of liturgy and pageantry which provide aesthetic clothing for worship. But the second group—those who look upon religion as an interpretation of life and a source of power for the battles of life—these are showing today a remarkable interest in drama and their interest has expressed itself in a rather amazing evolution in the use of dramatic forms in churches.

GROWING USE OF DRAMA IN AMERICAN CHURCHES

More than a thousand American churches now have dramatic groups. If Chicago churches are typical the number is much larger. For a recent study of the 276 churches in that city revealed that 216 of them were producing religious plays. Those 216 had produced 647 dramas and pageants in twelve months. Another recent survey, as already noted in the Introduction, discovered that of 364 churches in the Midwest, 322 produced 947 plays in the same period.

Most modern churches began with pageantry, presenting certain great ideas in the form of living pictures accompanied by music. But they did not stop with pageantry. They wanted to portray *character* and so they turned to drama which centers around character as pageantry centers around ideas. They dramatized Bible stories to help the children of the Sunday Schools to recover the experience of the old Bible characters and better to understand the struggles they went through. From Bible stories they passed on to revived mystery plays and to ancient and modern moralities. Next they developed plays of the mission fields, plays that have been a powerful aid in making real those fields and the struggles of our missionaries. But they could not stop there. The churches have now reached the place where they are asking for strong modern dramas, with humour and imagination, portraying the emotional and spiritual conflicts of human life, and shedding upon them the light of religion.

A NEW DEFINITION OF RELIGIOUS DRAMA

In this evolution the experience of the churches gradually gave a new definition to religious drama. In the beginning it was somehow felt that a religious drama must talk much about religion, and about Christ and the church; it must use biblical characters and to a large extent biblical stories. But in the course of the years we have come to see that what makes a play religious is not the material it deals with but *the total effect of the play upon the audience*. If a play sends an audience away exalted in spirit, with a deeper sense of fellowship with God and man, it has been religious. But if it does not have that effect it is not religious although all its characters are biblical and its story taken from the Bible itself. The churches have presented many an irreligious Bible play, and the theatres many a religious modern one. *Jephthah's Daughter* is a fair example of an irreligious biblical play, while Shaw's *St. Joan, Outward Bound* by Vane, *R.U.R.* by Capek, *Our Town*, by Thornton Wilder, *The Corn Is Green*, by Emlyn Williams, and *The Family Portrait*, by Coffee and Cowen are examples of modern plays that have a religious effect.

So much for the situation in the churches with regard to their own use of drama. They are not using drama to make money, nor as a new wrinkle in religious education, nor simply as a means of making Bible stories interesting to children. They are using it because they regard religion as a source of power for the struggles of human life and the drama as a means of interpreting those struggles artistically. *They are using it in a deliberate attempt to develop strength, beauty, and power in the imaginative and creative life of the players and the audiences*. It is no fad; its roots go down to the beginnings of religion and drama. Its immediate warrant lies in the need of our times for a spiritual ministry to the aesthetic and emotional life of our people. Its fruit is in human lives enriched in understanding, sympathy, and fellowship. No wonder, then, that Dr. Charles Clayton Morrison says, "The drama is destined to play an increasing part in the activities of the future parish."

THREE OUTSTANDING NEEDS IN RELIGIOUS DRAMA

What next? There are three outstanding needs in the area where religion and drama are working together. One is for more skill and insight in the production of religious dramas in churches and parish houses. The second is for more adequate equipment. This manual will not have been written in vain if it helps to meet these two needs. But the greatest need is for better plays. We have a few good plays—but *not half enough* to meet the demand. We want plays that are simple in their requirements for production and not beyond the ability of amateurs to play. But we want great plays for all that. Not propaganda plays. Not preachy plays. Not pious plays. We want plays of character and action, of humour and imagination, of beauty and power. Not plays that talk a lot about Christ, but plays with characters who do Christ-like deeds.

Is there some dramatist within the reach of these words? We write directly to him. Have you dreamed of some day writing a play so true to the deeper harmonies of human life that when people see it, it will start the bells ringing in their own hearts? Have you hoped to write a play in which you would put real characters under the pressure of such a crisis that it would break them open and show the souls within? Many of our playwrights have broken open their characters but found only a devil inside. Are you strong enough to break them deeper and find the divinity? Have you longed in your quiet moments for the insight and the ability to write a play so sympathetic with the hopes and frailties and aspirations of the common people that they will cherish it next their hearts as they cherish the poetry of Robert Burns? Write that play now and dedicate it to the young people of the churches who are learning through drama to reverence human personality as the temple of God. You may be the one of whom Dean Inge wrote. "When this new prophet comes," he said, "I think he will choose to speak to his generation not from the pulpit, nor from the platform, nor from the printed page, but from the stage. A great dramatist might help us find our souls."

The art of the drama is specially related to religion: the imagination is more powerfully affected and shaped by dramatic events than by anything else. Just as our private imaginations never quite cease to act over again certain "dramatic" experiences of our individual childhoods, so the imagination of a religious community is forever rehearsing again the sublime play between celestial and earthly beings from which it traces its origin, and in terms of this drama it understands its present world. . . .

One great advantage of seeking this imaginative understanding through religious drama is that, in proportion as it is acquired, it can influence not only our thoughts: it can influence our conception of what is happening in society. It can also sustain social courage in threatening times: for the Christian imagination conceiving how much we are living in the same drama in which Christ Himself lived and died, and how the same actors —Peter and Judas, Caiaphas, Pilate and the rest—are all in our world to-day in different guises, performing the same eternal drama, can also help us to realise that God is in it too, bringing about, in ways not our ways, worlds better than we could think out and design. And yet not so: but only in so far as there are individuals who live, rejoice, suffer and die, in the Spirit which, out of this greatest of human tragedies, arose triumphant in the end.

Philip Mairet

Chapter II

CHOOSING THE PLAY

DRAMA is the art of creating characters who convince us of their own true-to-life reality; of placing those characters in the midst of such conflicts as to throw their lives into a moment of intense crisis when they are faced with the necessity of making important choices between two or more possible solutions to the conflict; and then, through the decisions which the characters make and embody in their deeds, of revealing to the audience the characters' very souls.

Here is a day laborer who is out of a job. Day after day he has tramped the streets searching for work. At home are his wife and his little child. They are in desperate need. This day he comes home weary and discouraged only to hear the hungry cry of his child and to look into his wife's white, scared face. His wife shows him a well-filled purse that she has "found." Little by little he draws from her the story of how she stole it. She pleads with him to keep it, for their child's sake. He almost yields. But at last he rushes out with the purse in his hand and gives it to a policeman. That deed tells in no uncertain terms what that man's inmost character really is. The play is Alfred Sutro's *The Man on the Kerb.*

Character, convincingly shown by a *choice* made and a *deed* performed, at a time when the *struggle* is fierce and the *consequences* of utmost *importance*—this is the life stuff of all serious drama.

Yet these elements alone do not make a play. There must be a well-ordered story which will present these dramatic facts in such fashion as to compel interest and to stir emotional response in the audience. That is to say, every good play will have a skilfully contrived plot which will continually freshen interest in the action on the stage. More, it will hold the audience in a constant state of pleasurable suspense concerning the final outcome until the supreme moment of the play arrives. It will drop a hint here and there to whet curiosity, but always it will hold some decisive factor in reserve until the very last moment. Then, when the struggle finally ends on this long awaited peak of dramatic interest, the play itself will end and the curtain fall with no tag ends of the story left to drag on to anti-climax.

This emphasis upon a skilfully contrived plot must not, on the other hand, lead to the conclusion that a good play consists of a constant succession of new situations. The exact opposite is true. When one new situation follows another in rapid succession the dramatist has no time to mine each one deeply for its emotional values but is rather engrossed in the mere forward rush of outward events. This results in a bare chronicle whose speed cannot make up for its lack of depth. A play is to be considered as a progression of emotions rather than of events. The most successful plays are those in which the dramatist has succeeded in telling his story through a few well-planned major situations or episodes,[1] each one

[1] The term *episode*, as later defined in this manual, denotes that portion of the play which is carried on by one group of characters who are on the stage at any one time. When one of these characters leaves the group or another joins it, the center of interest shifts, and a new episode has begun.

of which is developed to its full emotional power. In a good one-act play there will seldom be more than eight episodes. Some of the best have only three to five.

Men are not satisfied, however, with a play which merely holds their attention and stirs their emotions for a brief hour or so. Even the perfect revelation of character is not enough. Men are incurably philosophical. They want their plays to make some revealing comment upon life which they can carry away with them and remember in days to come. Unless a play does this it fails to satisfy. Every good play has a clearly defined and worth-while theme which is not preached about but which, nevertheless, emerges clearly from the action. Thus, Sir James Barrie's play, *Dear Brutus*, is built around a quotation from Shakespeare's *Julius Caesar*,

> "The fault, dear Brutus, is not in our stars,
> But in ourselves, that we are underlings."

And Charles Rann Kennedy's *The Terrible Meek* brings out with vividness and power the truth of Jesus' saying, "Blessed are the meek, for they shall inherit the earth."

Moreover, the best plays are written by playwrights of imaginative grasp and power and are illuminated by flashes of humour. Great drama may and often does deal with some very sordid facts of life, but whether dealing with squalor or beauty it is never dull.

All of these prime dramatic qualities any play must have before it can command interest or move emotions profoundly. But the religious test still remains.

THE DECISIVE RELIGIOUS TEST

The religious value of any good play is determined solely by the total effect which it has upon the audience which sees it and the actors who produce it. The mere fact that a play happens to be biblical or that its characters chance to live in Palestine does not guarantee its religious nature. Nor does the fact that its locale is a mission field or a modern church.

But if, as a result of seeing the play, the men and women in the audience are lifted closer to God and inspired to go out and live more Christ-like lives, then the play is a religious play. So, too, with the actors. If the interpretation of their rôles broadens their sympathies and purifies their hearts by a sense of the sacredness of life, then the play is a religious play. Religious drama must meet this pragmatic test of the effect it has upon both audience and players before it is entitled to the name.

Here, then, is a series of tests which will help in choosing a worthy religious drama:

PRACTICAL TESTS FOR A RELIGIOUS DRAMA

I. Does it have the necessary dramatic strength?
  1. Does it reach the emotions?
     Unless a play moves the audience emotionally it is a failure, for the very definition of a play is that it is "an orderly representation of life arousing emotion in an audience" (Wilde).
  2. Do the characters seem real?
     The thing we remember longest in a play is not its plot or its theme, but its characters —at least one or two of them. A playwright's biggest task is to put one or more characters under the pressure of a great crisis

and under that pressure to break them open so that their very souls are revealed.

3. Is the conflict adequate?

Much of the interest in drama depends upon the clash of wills and personalities. If the central characters were not put under the pressure of such a conflict, the playwright could not break them open so that the audience could see what kind of persons they are.

4. Does the conflict rise to a climax?

If it does not, it will not hold the interest of the audience.

5. Is the suspense sustained?

Otherwise both interest and emotions lag.

6. Do the characters have to make important choices?

The bigger the central choice in a play, the bigger the play tends to be. Hamlet's "to be or not to be" is a sample of an important choice. Moreover, characters and personalities are revealed largely by the choices they make.

7. Is the theme clear and worth while?

Every work of art is an illustration and a working out of a certain central idea.

8. Is the solution convincing?

The result of the struggle must not be left in doubt. It must issue logically and convincingly from the reaction of the characters to their situation and not simply represent the manipulation of the author.

9. Does the play reveal a struggle common to the experience of the audience?

If it does not, the audience will have but an academic and detached interest in it.

10. Does the play present contrasting moods?

These make for lights and shadows in a play. While not so essential in a one-act play, they yet add interest and liveliness.

11. Does it have a well-knit episodic structure?

A play is built out of episodes, each one of which has its own dramatic situation, conflict, purpose, and emotional reaction. The better plays have few episodes each mined deeply for emotional values rather than many mined superficially. A one-act play divided into several scenes requiring change of setting loses emotional continuity. Many one-act plays fail here.

II. Does the play have a religious effect?

1. Does it have a religious effect upon the audience?

That is, does it send the audience away exalted in spirit and with a deeper sense of fellowship with God and man?

2. Does it have a religious effect upon the actors?

That is, does the interpretation of their parts call for such study and sympathetic insight as will broaden their sympathies and ennoble their souls.

III. Does the play lie within the possibilities of production by the group planning to present it?

1. Are the scenic and lighting effects required such as can be supplied by the equipment at hand? Are more stage sets required than the group can effectively create?

2. Is the costuming simple or elaborate? How

much will it cost in time and labor to costume this play?

3. Is the character portrayal necessary within the ability of the actors who will take part?

TYPES OF RELIGIOUS DRAMA

There are five varieties or types of religious drama each having its own function and value: (1) the prepared play, such as is contemplated in the above discussion; (2) the dramatized Bible story; (3) the pageant; (4) the visualization; and (5) the liturgical drama.

The Prepared Play

This is the well-constructed religious drama freely fashioned after the plan of all good drama whether religious or secular. Such a play may deal with biblical characters or modern and its action may be laid in any setting under the sun which the author is able to make convincing. Edna Baldwin's *Ba Thane* is an example of a prepared play which deals with life on a modern mission field; Mary Hamlin's *The Rock* and *He Came Seeing* of ones which deal with New Testament figures; Fred Eastman's *Bread* and *Our Lean Years* of ones which deal with life in rural America.

The field of the prepared play offers the church today the widest range of choice and contains, for adults, by far the most powerful religious drama available. In general, the prepared play will be found most appropriate for presentation in the parish house, though occasionally one is found which has such a distinctly worshipful atmosphere that it may be given in the church auditorium.

The Dramatized Bible Story

This form consists of the relatively unelaborated portrayal of a biblical narrative just as it stands. When the form is at its best the story will, of course, be presented with all of the dramatic possibilities of the original text fully developed, yet the plot and characterization will, of necessity, be limited to the simple set of facts given or implied in the biblical source. Thus, in dramatizing the Christmas story, a group of children would show Mary and Joseph lodged in the stable with the infant Jesus, the coming of the shepherds, and then of the wise men. Beyond this simple set of characters and ordering of events they could not go in a simple dramatization of the New Testament narrative.

The prepared play on the other hand might tell the Christmas story in altogether different fashion. Elizabeth McFadden, for instance, in her *Tidings of Joy* puts the story in a modern setting in the home of a young couple faced with eviction but befriended by persons animated by the Christmas spirit. Marion Wefer's *A King Shall Reign* lays the scene in the home of a sorrowing Jewish mother whose hope is renewed by Joseph and Mary and their babe on their flight to Egypt.

The chief use of the simple, dramatized Bible story is to help the pupils recover the experience of the Bible characters and to understand better the struggles they went through. It is a very effective way of presenting these classic stories of our religion and of emphasizing their teachings. The dramatized Bible story probably rises to its highest degree of usefulness among the children of the church school when they are led in working out their own dramatizations. Such a project calls upon the child for the use of his sympathetic imagination in the study of the biblical character he is attempting to portray. It also calls upon him for a study of the times and their customs and awakens his creative instinct in the attempt to reproduce and interpret them. Mrs. Elizabeth Erwin Miller has had marked success in leading children in such dramatizations. The following outline of the method which she uses in such work is taken from her book, *The Dramatization of Biblical Stories* (The University of Chicago Press).

How to Dramatize a Bible Story

"1. Select a story with care; then adapt it for telling.

2. Tell the story, emphasizing the essential parts.

3. Let the children divide the story into pictures or scenes.

4. Have a discussion of what should take place in each scene.

5. Let volunteers from among the children act out one scene as they think it should be done, using their own words.

6. Develop criticism by the other children with suggestions for improvement.

7. Have a second acting of the scene for improvement.

8. Let each of the other scenes be worked out in the same manner.

9. See that every child has the chance to try out many parts.

10. Play the story through many times. Change it often according to criticism, until the children recognize the result as a product of their best effort.

11. With the help of the children change the words into biblical form.

12. Let the group assign definite parts to be learned for the final performance."

Occasionally a dramatized Bible story may be used in an adult service of worship with good effect. Experience shows, however, that the form is generally inferior in emotional power to the work of a good dramatist.

A more extended treatment of creative dramatics applied to Bible stories will be found in Winifred Ward's *Creative Dramatics*, Hulda Niebuhr's *Ventures in Drama*, and R. W. Raine's *Bible Dramatics*.

The Pageant

The pageant seeks to give a beautiful and impressive presentation of some history or idea by means of a climactic series of stage pictures accompanied by interpretative music. It may or may not have dialogue but it should always have action and a forward flow of events. The pageant differs from the drama proper in two ways:

First, the pageant is concerned primarily with *ideas* rather than with *characters*. It deals with the sweep of some phase of history or the growth of some institution or social movement. It is not woven together, as is the drama proper, of the struggles of a particular individual whose well-defined character, through some revealing act of his own will, determines the outcome.

Second, the pageant has only a *loose plot*. In the drama our interest is sustained by a single series of related events rising toward a climax. Each one of these events is determined in its outcome by the inner nature of the characters involved. It is this clearly portrayed series of consequences flowing from character-revealing choices and deeds of real men and women which holds our interest breathless to the end. But in the pageant we have merely a series of related episodes arranged in climactic sequence. A closely knit plot is impossible in a dramatic form in which the development of an idea rather than the development of a particular character is stressed.

On the other hand, the pageant uses more participants than a play, it usually creates a more spectacular effect and if the music is well chosen and executed it combines an appeal of color and sound that may be very effective. Moreover, the pageant may rise to heights of spiritual power, as witness George Pierce Baker's *Pageant of the Pilgrim Spirit*.

But exactly because its primary emphasis is upon ideas rather than characters it is seldom that it can equal the drama proper in its religious effect upon an audience. Men are always moved most deeply when the idea is made flesh in the person of a well-drawn human character. In the drama proper they can become intimately acquainted with such a character and follow with uninterrupted interest through all the struggle and suspense of a closely woven plot until his soul-revealing choice is at last made.

However, all of this is not to deny the pageant its own proper sphere of usefulness. In the total dramatic program of the church year there always come times when some anniversary is to be celebrated. At such times what is wanted is not, perhaps, a drama unified about the characters of some one particular time and place but rather a presentation of the entire forward movement of the institution over a long period of years. Then only the pageant will do. Or it may be that the poetry of some season such as the Christmastide will master the heart. Then perhaps the congregation will want to escape from the limitations of the particular and for a time delight itself in the free realm of fancy and of pictorial and musical beauty. If so a pageant is the thing to choose. Although this manual is not concerned directly with the production of the pageant, yet it may be well to indicate briefly certain tests of a pageant's worth. These may be used both in helping to choose the pageant wisely and in guiding to its adequate production. These special tests for the pageant should be considered, so far as possible, along with the standards already given for choosing a religious drama proper.

Tests to be Applied to a Pageant

1. *Theme*

   Does the pageant have a clearly defined theme which is both noble and appropriate?

2. *Structure*

   Does each episode carry on this theme, developing and enriching it? In a well-constructed pageant there should be, as a general rule, not less than three nor more than seven episodes, and the entire number should be arranged in a unified and climactic sequence. No one episode should require more than twenty-five minutes. Each should contain the dramatic elements of suspense, choice, characterization, conflict, and the power of arousing the sympathy of the hearer for one character or another.

3. *Treatment*

   Is the treatment simple and clear, yet sufficiently varied to hold the interest of the audience throughout? Is there a carefully balanced and rhythmic correlation of the elements of movement, action, speech, music, pictorial effect, dancing, lighting, costuming, and symbolism?

4. *Movement*

   Is the pageant simply a static collection of pictures or tableaux or does it move forward to a climax?

5. *Action*

   Does the action in each episode follow the tempo

implied by the type of episode and is it characteristic and significant?

6. *Text*

   Is the text accurate historically and illuminated by local color? Is the dialogue short, clear, natural, and pointed? Is the text as a whole dignified, rhythmic, and euphonious, with only such exceptions as are necessary for contrast and character portrayal?

7. *Music*

   Has the music been specifically selected and designated by the author and does it truly accentuate and interpret the changing moods of the piece? Is it purposeful, sincere, emotionally expressive, appropriate to the words with which it is used, and characteristic of the time of its use?

8. *Pictorial Effect*

   Are the stage pictures always characteristic, and of good composition and harmonious coloring?

9. *Dancing*

   Does the dancing truly convey ideas and moods? Dances should stimulate emotional response and help set the tempo for the pageant as a whole.

10. *Lighting*

    Does the lighting illuminate and unify the pictures as a whole and at the same time emphasize their salient features?

11. *Costuming*

    Is the costuming characteristic, colorful, and harmonious?

12. *Symbolism*

    Is the symbolism fresh, original, clear, yet delicate and subtle?

The Visualization

Under this classification come most of the propaganda playlets whose chief function is to convey information about missions or temperance or the safety movement or a hundred other branches of education and social service. Occasionally one finds a skilfully constructed piece of this sort, but most of such material now in print is so inartistically done and so loaded with propaganda and data that it does not deserve serious consideration.

The Liturgical Drama

A liturgical drama is one written to be played in the chancel of the church with no other setting than that provided by the choir and sanctuary; a drama intended, in itself, to be an act of worship. In this category is the Mass, but here also are many of the old miracle and mystery plays such as those which Phillips E. Osgood has adapted for modern use to be played before the altar. Here, too, would be any play whose entire structure and idea content have been shaped to the environment of the chancel and whose presentation is intended to be an act of worship.

There are very few good plays of this type available, although this is perhaps the only type which may be offered in the church itself with complete artistic consistency. Most religious plays are best fitted for production in the parish house. It is to be hoped that more dramatic writers may be led to see the possibilities inherent in this form and to give us more true worship-dramas of a worthy nature. The liturgical drama, ideally, may have all of the emotional strength and spiritual power possible in the prepared play. In actuality, however, it is all too apt to suffer from those weaknesses inherent in the pageant form, abstractness of ideas and lack of plot interest.

The matter of royalties will come up—and stay up—with every choice of a new play. The arguments against royalties are obvious: the play is being given for religious purposes and not for commercial profit; no admission will be charged; the treasury is empty; etc., etc. A large proportion of the mail of authors and publishers is filled with these arguments coupled with requests to cancel the royalties upon certain plays.

On the other hand, authors and publishers reply, Do you expect your preacher to preach without salary? Or your makers of hymnbooks to supply them without charge because they are to be used in a religious service? The writing of a good play requires weeks, often months, of hard work. The profit on the sale of the paper-backed copies of the play is small or non-existent. *Practically the only return the author and publisher receive for their labor is from the royalties.* The publishers go on to say that when a church wishes hymnbooks it buys one for every member or family. But when it produces a play it buys (and rightly) only one for each member of the producing group. Thus the sale of the book of a play is exceedingly limited and the difference must be made up in royalties.

Such are the arguments. Suppose a group thinks that its own arguments against royalties are so strong that it decides against a royalty play and chooses a non-royalty one. Immediately it discovers that, with few exceptions, it has only inferior plays from which to select. Church boards have published scores of plays in behalf of missions and other enterprises of the church and these are available without royalties. But most of them are loaded to the muzzle with propaganda or preachment, and so weak in artistic technique that no amount of painstaking work on the part of the group can make an audience feel that it has seen a good drama.

If, however, the decision is made to produce a royalty play in spite of the lean treasury, the group discovers two results: a greater enthusiasm on the part of the cast as they work on the better play, and a more inspiring response from the audience. The greater response of the audience is registered in larger offerings and in increased attendance. The testimony of most amateur groups has been overwhelming to the effect that they began the production of royalty plays with bated breath wondering if they could possibly afford it, but the experience of two or three years justified the hazard. Most groups that decided against royalty plays did not last two or three years.

This is not to say that all royalties are just. A royalty of five dollars for a one-act play and fifteen to twenty-five for a three-act play has proven quite within the bounds of possibility even for the small community. It is an investment in *quality* as well as a fair compensation to author and publisher. But royalty alone does not guarantee quality. Unless a play registers positively to the tests suggested in the earlier part of this chapter it had better be left upon the shelf.

HOW ABOUT THE COST?

Religious drama can and should be self-supporting, once the original stage and equipment are provided. The secret lies in (a) choosing strong plays and giving them good productions; (b) securing, through effective publicity, congregations large enough to assure free will offerings of ten to twenty dollars; (c) economical business management; (d) repeat performances in neighboring churches; and (e) care of costumes and properties, building up wardrobe and equipment for future use. Details of these items will be considered in the following chapters. But we may close this one with an extract from a letter describing how one church has made its drama self-supporting by this method:

"You may be interested in knowing the plays we have produced to date: *The Terrible Meek, The Valiant, Dust of the Road, And He Came to His Father, The Confessional, The Doctor Decides* (one each month). The attendance has been constantly growing and at the last play it was necessary to move chairs into the church auditorium—and even then, some of the congregation had to stand in the vestibule. The night *Dust of the Road* was presented the temperature was below zero, and yet over two hundred people attended. You will note that we started with one of the strongest plays possible on the assumption that its success or failure would determine our success or failure during the balance of the winter. It was also selected because of the simplicity of the setting and the small number of parts. We produced *The Doctor Decides* again last Sunday night in another town and it was well received—we met expenses and the minister informed us it was one of the biggest congregations he had had all winter. To date we have spent $25 for royalties and have a balance of $20 in the treasury—we take a collection at each play. If there is still a balance this spring, we shall try to improve our stage equipment, anticipating an even more successful program next winter."

Chapter III

ORGANIZATION FOR PRODUCTION

HOW *NOT* TO DO IT

A CHURCH-DRAMA group has selected Mary P. Hamlin's fine drama of New Testament times, *He Came Seeing*. The cast has spent weeks of conscientious rehearsal upon it and at last the night of its production has come. The enveloping service of worship was begun promptly at eight o'clock according to schedule and its carefully planned sequence of instrumental prelude, prayer, Scripture reading and hymn has proceeded until the audience is now emotionally prepared to receive the message of the play.

But backstage there is a terrible to-do. It has been discovered at the last moment that the little copper bowl which Joab, the blind youth of the play, is to use is missing. Joab had always used one of the church's wooden collection plates during the rehearsals. No one has remembered to get a real bowl for tonight. There has been a hurried council of war and Joab has dashed off in a car to get a copper bowl from Mary Smith's house. He should be back by now, but he may have had a puncture and had to change a tire. The entire cast is nervous and upon the verge of a quarrel trying to settle whose fault the oversight has been. The minister is called to one side and told of the trouble. He speaks words of confidence to soothe taut nerves and returns to fill in the gap in the service by an extempore choice of hymns.

At last Joab arrives with his bowl. Someone sticks a head out between the curtains and nods to the minister that the players are ready. The congregational singing is brought to a close and the curtains then part upon the opening scene of the play. However, the lights in the auditorium are still on so that much of the effect is lost until one of the ushers makes his way to the switchboard and turns off the house lights. Meanwhile the audience has grown restless and a woman down front is complaining audibly of the lack of ventilation. The players themselves are in anything but a devotional mood. Consequently they are giving an interpretation whose level is much below that of the last rehearsal. Yet the inherent power of the play itself at last begins to grip both players and audience. The play seems about to come to its close with a considerable degree of strength. And then, in the last impressive pause while Joab struggles with his decision, an inexperienced prompter pressed into service at the last moment grows nervous over the pause and prompts in a voice audible over the entire auditorium. The curtains close while players and audience alike breathe a sigh of relief.

But the story is not yet told. Six weeks later the minister receives two irate calls over his telephone. One is from Mary Smith's mother demanding to know when her copper bowl is to be returned. The other is from a local printer who wants to know when his bill for certain printed programs for the play is to be paid.

WHAT WAS WRONG?

A strong, beautiful play upon which weeks of rehearsal have been spent has been utterly ruined. Both players and audience have been depressed, and business obligations have been neglected, all because of what? Just one thing—the lack of *proper organization and distribution of responsibilities* at the very beginning of work upon the play.

Undertaking the production of a worthy religious play involves many obligations:

To the audience the producing group owes that care and foresight which will insure its physical comfort and freedom from distraction during the service of worship of which the play is a part. This may seem elementary, but it is essential. Physical discomfort and distracting noise or lighting can destroy the atmosphere of worship as surely as can poor acting in the play itself.

To the players the group owes such careful and clearly defined distribution of individual responsibilities that they may work together efficiently and without irritation. The players have a right to experience the religious uplift which follows when they each and all, assuming their responsible parts in a group enterprise, come to feel that through that cooperative effort a beautiful thing is being created, that through their common, brotherly effort God is speaking a message to the souls of men. More, the group, through its director, owes each player such help in the understanding and interpretation of his rôle that his own imagination and human sympathies may be broadened by his living with the character he portrays.

To the author the group owes a fine and true interpretation of his play. And to both author and publisher it owes a prompt and businesslike meeting of all royalty obligations.

To all with whom the group deals during its work upon the play, whether it be the printer who prints the programs, the person from whom it borrows properties, or the janitor who cares for the hall where it holds its rehearsals, it owes such consideration and such conscientious meeting of its obligations as shall bring honor to the term Christian.

Needless to say, these many obligations will not be fulfilled if left to chance. The successful production of a play requires a degree of careful organization and an exact placing of responsibilities approaching that found in military life.

First of all such a group needs a director. He should be appointed by the church and given absolute authority over the entire production. Since the drama is to be an artistic production, it must have unity and there is no better way of making the finished product a unit than by having its director a unit, that is, an individual rather than a committee or a group. It is to be hoped that he will be a benevolent dictator, sympathetic and eager to receive suggestions, but a dictator he must be if he is to have the responsibility for the complete production.

A PRACTICAL PLAN OF ORGANIZATION

The next step is for the director to form a production organization with a differentiation of labor such as follows:

Assistant Director: To help the director and conduct rehearsals in the director's absence. Responsible also for the creation and harmonizing of other items on the program with the play, such as the enveloping service of worship.

Business Manager: Responsible for all business arrangements, secures engagements, stage, ushers, programs, keeps full and accurate account of all receipts and expenditures, and renders a complete report to the director a day after the production. The business manager is also responsible for seeing that the house is well ventilated and free from disturbing noises during rehearsals as well as during productions.

Publicity Manager: Responsible for securing the audience. To this end he writes publicity and advertising and places it, makes speeches, and does everything else his ingenuity suggests in order to assure the cast an adequate audience.

Stage Manager: Responsible for stage sets, draperies, curtains, the placement of major properties, and the cleanliness and order of all things back of the front curtain.

Electrician: Responsible for both stage and house lights and their manipulation to secure the right effects.

Property Manager: Makes a list of necessary properties, secures them, sees that they are in their proper places on the stage, and returns them to their owners promptly after production.

Costume Manager: Responsible for securing proper costumes, having them ready at least one week before production and returned promptly on the day following production.

Make-up Manager: Responsible for make-up of the cast. Must work in harmony with costume manager and electrician to secure harmonious effects.

Prompter: Holds the book of the play through rehearsals as well as during production.

Such a plan of organization will give satisfactory results for the occasional production of a single play or pageant and will be all that is needed. However, if the church plans to make the use of the religious drama a regular part of its program, much more satisfaction will be gained through the further organization of a religious drama club. Through such an organization the interest of a larger number of people can be enlisted permanently in the dramatic program of the church. Moreover, its standing officers and committees save much of the fuss incident to the necessity for organizing each play in entire isolation from those that precede and those that follow. Perhaps most important of all, such a club offers a means through which a serious study of the drama can be promoted and its significance constantly seen in relation to the total program and mission of the Church. Through this organization, the players can meet regularly to read and discuss good plays and to think through the problems of their artistic staging.

The following model constitution may prove helpful in the organization of such a permanent dramatic group.

CONSTITUTION FOR A RELIGIOUS DRAMA CLUB

The purpose of this club is twofold: first, to enable its members, through the study of the best plays, to enlarge their sympathetic understanding of both the individual and social struggles of men, and to strengthen their imaginative grasp upon the full meaning of the Christian way of life; second, to produce from time to time such plays as will constitute, both for the players and the audience, a religious experience.

The membership of this club shall consist of all adults who shall signify their intention to become members through entering their names upon the secretary's roll of the club membership and through taking part in the activities of the club.

The club shall meet in *weekly session* for the group study of plays and of matters connected with their artistic production.

The club shall hold *quarterly business meetings* for the determination of questions of policy and for hearing reports from the director and business manager and approving or disapproving of the same. A formal report of their work shall be due from each of these officers at every quarterly business meeting of the club, as well as from the treasurer.

Special business meetings may be called at the discretion of the president.

The following *officers* shall be elected at the first regular business meeting of each church year and shall hold office until the corresponding meeting of the next church year: president, vice-president, secretary, business manager, and director.

The duties of the *president* shall consist of presiding over the quarterly business meetings and all called meetings. He shall also appoint the members of all standing committees and shall be the public representative of the club at the presentation of the plays, etc., and in giving out to the public signed announcements of club affairs.

The duties of the president shall devolve upon the *vice-president* in the absence or incapacity of the president.

The duties of the *secretary* shall be to keep the minutes of all business meetings of the club, to maintain an accurate roll of its membership, and to conduct all necessary correspondence.

The duties of the *business manager* shall be to keep in trust all money received by the club and to pay such money out only upon the signed requisitions of the director. The business manager shall also keep an accurate account of all money received into his keeping and of sums paid out by him. He shall have complete charge of and responsibility for all business affairs of the club in periods between the regular or called business meetings.

The duties of the *director* shall be to take complete charge of the plays produced by the club, selecting the casts, organizing and distributing responsibilities, conducting rehearsals, and exercising final control over the work of all committees and persons directly contributing to the work of producing plays. He shall also conduct the weekly study sessions of the club.

The following standing committee as well as the group of officers listed below shall be appointed by the president within a week after his taking office. These committeemen and appointive officers shall function until their successors are appointed by the next president, save only that the president may, at his discretion, dismiss any or all such persons who fail to perform their duties and appoint others to the vacant posts.

1. *A committee on the selection of plays* for production. This committee shall consist of five members and shall be charged with the responsibility for selecting plays for production by the club. The director shall be an ex-officio member of this committee.

2. *A costume manager* and one or more assistants. This costume manager shall be charged with the responsibility for costuming all plays produced by the club.

3. *A stage manager* and one or more assistants. This stage manager shall be responsible for the design and management of all stage sets, for all rehearsals and productions.

4. *A property manager* and one or more assistants. This property manager shall be responsible for the collection and return of all properties necessary for productions and rehearsals.

5. *An electrician* and one or more assistants. This electrician shall be charged with the responsibility of artistic stage lighting and the proper handling of house lighting for all productions.

6. *A publicity manager*. This publicity manager shall be charged with the responsibility of advertising the productions through verbal announcements, church bulletins, newspapers, posters, etc.[1]

[1] *Note:* In the above model constitution a make-up manager is not listed among the appointive officers. This is because, in a permanently organized dramatic group, it is desirable that the entire club study the art of make-up. This can be carried out as a project in the weekly study sessions. It is then sufficient that the director check the effect of each individual's make-up at the dress rehearsal.

Chapter IV

DIRECTING

UPON the director's shoulders rests the responsibility for molding together all of the diverse elements which go to make up the play until one artistic whole is achieved. He must give to the production unity, coherence, and emphasis. He must see that from beginning to end the performance is at all times both pleasing and convincing, that it seizes and holds the interest of the audience, and that the message of the play is brought out with compelling emotional power. A job of this magnitude requires a systematic approach.

GETTING OFF TO A GOOD START

Let the first thing which the director does be to study the play carefully, noting its theme and mood, its structure and its characters. Then let him call the entire group of actors together and read the play to them.

Following this he will lead the group in a discussion during which these points will be made clear: (1) the central theme; (2) the personalities of the various characters and the nature of the struggle in which each one is engaged; (3) the religious effects which the play should have upon its audience; and (4) the dramatic structure. This last point will include a discussion of the place at which the play reaches its climax, the nature of the final crisis or solution, and the reason for each episode or scene together with its relation to the other episodes.

Next, let the director give each member of the group a copy of the play for individual study. Let him also announce the time and purpose of the next meeting. Its nature will be a trial reading of portions of the play by members of the group and its purpose that of enabling the director to choose the cast.

This first meeting should give the members an intelligent grasp of the play. More, through observation of the way in which the members enter into the discussion, it should give the director an opportunity to judge of their sympathetic grasp of the play and of their understanding of its characters.

CHOOSING THE CAST

At the next meeting let the group arrange itself in chairs placed in a circle. The director will then ask various members to read certain of the most important lines in the different parts without any attempt at business. After he has satisfied himself as to which players are best suited for the parts he will announce his decision, making it clear that he is passing no judgment upon the others, and that those who receive the important parts in this play must be prepared to accept minor ones in the next play.

In making these choices the director will of course bear many things in mind. He will consider the general physical fitness and adaptability of the player to the particular rôle under consideration, the quality and pitch of his voice, his age in comparison with the supposed age of the character to be portrayed, his apparent emotional grasp of the part, his ability to give an intelligent and discriminating reading of the lines, and, last but by no means least, his attitude toward the group—his ability to cooperate as a unit in a group enterprise demanding a high order of dependability and an almost military discipline.

The fundamental quality of a player's voice is an important thing to bear in mind, for while incorrect pronunciation and careless enunciation may be corrected, it is disastrous to place a player with a squeaky voice in a rôle demanding deep-voiced dignity. The need for general physical adaptability to the demands of the part speaks for itself. As to age, the most convincing results are achieved when youths can be cast as youths and older men as older men. Emotional grasp and intelligence are highly important. Experience is usually desirable if the rôle is exacting, but this consideration should not bear too much weight if the other factors are favorable. Dependability and a cooperative spirit, however, are prime requisites.

SCHEDULING REHEARSALS

At this second meeting the director should also announce a complete schedule of rehearsals, including the definite time and place of each. He should ask each member of this newly chosen cast to make a careful copy of this schedule and he should make it very clear that every person who accepts a place in the cast gives an implicit pledge to be at every rehearsal and to be there on time. One member of a cast even a few minutes late wastes the time of every other person connected with the play. Persons who will not take this responsibility seriously should not be cast. It will be well, also, if this schedule lists a definite objective for each rehearsal. The number of rehearsals necessary for the successful production of a play will of course vary according to the length and difficulty of the play chosen and the experience of the players. *However, it will be necessary always to hold at least six rehearsals for a one-act play and fifteen for a three-act play.* Nor should these rehearsals be spaced too far apart. Two two-hour rehearsals each week give satisfactory results. For whatever suggestive value they may have, there are given here two such schedules of rehearsals, the first for a one-act, the second for a three-act play.

REHEARSAL SCHEDULE FOR A ONE-ACT PLAY

Tuesday, September 6, 8 p.m.—
Walk through the play with scripts in hand establishing stage positions and movements. Go through the play twice.

Friday, September 9, 8 p.m.—
Work for convincing characterizations and clear vocal effects. Players may still use their scripts.

Tuesday, September 13, 8 p.m.—
No scripts allowed on the stage. Players should know their lines. All details of the stage setting as well as all properties ready for use. Concentrate on characterization and clear vocal effects.

Friday, September 16, 8 p.m.—
Heighten the conflicts.

Tuesday, September 20, 8 p.m.—
Work for quickness in picking up cues and for group playing. In costume, with full lighting effects.

Friday, September 23, 8 p.m.—
Work for correct tempo, for continuity and smoothness. In costume, with full lighting effects and make-up.

Sunday, September 25, 8 p.m.—
  Public production.

REHEARSAL SCHEDULE FOR A THREE-ACT PLAY

Tuesday, November 1, 8 p.m.—
  Walk through first act with scripts in hand establishing stage positions and movements. Go through the act twice.

Friday, November 4, 8 p.m.—
  Review first act. Walk through second act with scripts in hand establishing stage positions and movements. Go through this act twice.

Tuesday, November 8, 8 p.m.—
  Review second act. Walk through third act with scripts in hand establishing stage positions and movements. Go through this act twice.

Friday, November 11, 8 p.m.—
  First act without scripts. Review second and third acts. All hand properties ready.

Tuesday, November 15, 8 p.m.—
  First two acts without scripts. Review third act.

Friday, November 18, 8 p.m.—
  Entire play without scripts.

Tuesday, November 22, 8 p.m.—
  Entire play. Concentrate on characterization. All stage sets ready.

Friday, November 25, 8 p.m.—
  Entire play. Concentrate on securing clear vocal effects. Drill on proper volume and clear enunciation.

Tuesday, November 29, 8 p.m.—
  Entire play. Emphasize the conflicts.

Friday, December 2, 8 p.m.—
  Entire play. Work for quickness on cues and group playing.

Tuesday, December 6, 8 p.m.—
  Drill on difficult passages in first two acts.

Friday, December 9, 8 p.m.—
  Concentrate on third act.

Tuesday, December 13, 8 p.m.—
  Entire play for tempo, continuity, and smoothness.

Friday, December 16, 8 p.m.—
  Entire play for tempo, continuity, and smoothness. In costume with full lighting effects.

Tuesday, December 20, 8 p.m.—
  Entire play for tempo, continuity, and smoothness. In costume with full lighting effects and make-up.

Wednesday, December 21, 8 p.m.—
  Public production.

WORKING OUT THE STAGE PLOTS

Between the second meeting when the cast is selected and the schedule announced and the date of the first actual rehearsal, the director and stage manager should lay out a plot of the stage and the properties. This should show the location of all windows, entrances, exits, furniture, and other set properties. The director and the assistant director will then go through the manuscript and indicate at their proper places the movement of the characters, the business, the crossings, and the changes in lighting. Perhaps the most practical way to work out the movement and crosses is to make the plot of the stage and its furnishings of considerable size. The director will lay this plot flat upon his desk. Next he will write the names of the various characters upon little squares of cardboard. Now, by moving the cardboard squares about over the plot of the stage as the action of the play is worked out, he can readily visualize the groupings which will result. If, however, the effect is not altogether pleasing when actually seen upon the stage, minor adjustments may readily be made during the first rehearsals. The important thing is to have the action plotted beforehand as perfectly as possible. This will save time in rehearsals and win the respect of the actors.

It will be well for the director to draw simple diagrams of these stage groupings and movements upon every page of his director's manuscript. Each diagram will show the floor plan of the stage and its furnishings in simple outline and will use the initial letters of the various characters' names to indicate their positions. Movement can be indicated by arrows, thus:

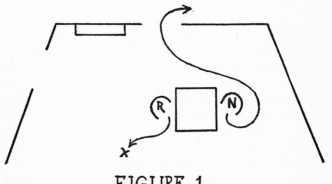

FIGURE 1
HOW TO RECORD MOVEMENT

These diagrams may be done, thumb-nail fashion, on the wide margins of the text, or, better, the text may be interleaved with blank pages. Upon these blank pages should also be noted the cues for light changes, and the operation of off-stage effects.

GROUPING

After the action has been blocked out, the director then checks its validity by observing the grouping he has produced. The picture in the frame of the stage should have good composition and be well balanced. The director must avoid having the actors block the audience's vision of the other actors. He must not overcrowd the stage on one side or the other. The grouping should always bear a direct relationship to the mental attitudes of the characters to each other. If one man, for example, is in mental conflict with three others, the director will have this opposition shown by his grouping, placing the antagonists on one side and the protagonist on the other. He will further strive to arrange his groupings so that all important actions may take place on important and easily visible parts of the stage. And he will contrive to secure a fairly constant flow of movement. A static stage is uninteresting. Even scenes wherein characters do nothing but carry on a lengthy conversation can be broken up by natural movements about the stage through the exercise of a little ingenuity. And, lastly, all groupings and movements must appear to issue from logical causes. There must be an apparent reason for every movement which the actor makes.

ENTRANCES

In plotting the action the matter of entrances deserves special consideration. Downstage entrances [1] are weak because the character must usually advance several steps upon the stage before he attracts the attention of the entire audience. Upstage entrances, on the other hand, are strong because they command every eye as soon as made. An entrance from upstage center is the strongest of all. Important characters should be given strong entrances, the more so because the playwright usually gives them important entrance lines.

THE IMPORTANCE OF THE EPISODE

The first lesson which the wise director will learn in regard to rehearsals is the importance of rehearsing by episodes. The episode is that portion of the action which is carried forward by any one group of characters who are upon the stage at any one time. Episodes are the fundamental units of the play's structure. If each of these units is not strong the whole will fall. Every episode will have some element of conflict between the characters involved which will rise to its own climax somewhere near the close and then shade off in preparation for the succeeding episode. Unless each of the lesser climaxes is thus brought out and all are kept in their relative importance, the play as a whole cannot gain the increasing interest of the audience and its suspense until the final curtain.

[1] Downstage is toward the audience. Upstage is away from the audience toward the rear of the stage. Stage left and right are at the left and right *of the actor* as he stands at the center of the stage facing the audience. Stage center is self-explanatory. Upstage center is a point upstage and midway between extreme stage left and right.

The director should, therefore, at the first regular rehearsal, have the group mark the episode divisions in their scripts. He should then ask the characters involved in each separate episode to fix upon certain times aside from the regular rehearsals of the full cast when they can meet and work toward perfecting their episodes. This intensive work upon the individual episodes will do more than any other one thing toward making the play a success. The work of conducting the episode rehearsals may be left in the hands of the assistant director. But the director himself should have a report of the number of such rehearsals held and the progress made. To this end he will give to the assistant director a blank rehearsal record (see Figure 2, page 57) to be filled out as the rehearsals are held and kept for the director's inspection at times of regular rehearsals.

When the hour of rehearsal comes let the director make it clear that the time for social pleasantries has ceased. There should be no distracting off-stage conversation or noise. Each player should be alert to do his part promptly and well, every mind concentrated upon this one thing—the success of the play. Every member of the production organization should be held to strict accountability for the prompt performance of his responsibilities. The hour of rehearsal is a time for serious business. It will help to develop atmosphere if, during the entire period of the rehearsal, every player be called only by the name of the character he is portraying. Players should be urged to keep themselves in the spirit of their characterizations even while waiting off-stage.

At the opening of each rehearsal let the director call all of the players together and briefly yet clearly outline the things which he wishes accomplished. There may also be a few special bits of counsel for particular players before the work is actually begun, such as, "Remember to keep up the volume of your voice today, Peter, and to give full value to your final consonants. I couldn't hear you at the back of the room at our last rehearsal," or, "Watch that long scene where you have no speeches, Deborah. Don't drop out of character just because you have nothing to say." Then the rehearsal will begin.

The prompter should be on the job at every single rehearsal. The director should never have to watch the text of the play in order to prompt. His attention is needed upon the stage for matters of interpretation.

After the first rehearsals for blocking out the action and establishing the stage business have been left behind, the flow of the play should be interrupted as little as possible. The director will keep a notebook in his hand and jot down his criticisms of the players in that as the play goes on. Then, at the close of an episode which has gone faultily, he will call the players back on the stage and make his suggestions. If there is time they may then do the entire episode over, bearing his criticism in mind. Otherwise they should take note and remember his criticism while studying for the next rehearsal. Occasionally it is necessary to break in upon an episode to give some specific suggestion, but, so far as possible, the director should work for continuity of action and steady flow of the emotional tides of the play from the very first. Only in this way can the play achieve a strong, unified effect and

REHEARSAL SCHEDULE

"ETERNAL LIFE"

By Fred Eastman

Pages of script	Feb. 11. Blocking out, grouping and reading	Feb. 13. Characterization, enunciation and voice	Feb. 18. Characterization, props, mood, conflicts, quick cues	Feb. 20. No scripts, conflicts, timing, interrelation of characters	Feb. 25. No scripts, pantomime tempo, rhythm, quick cues, costumes	Feb. 27. No scripts, tempo, rhythm, climax, polishing, costumes, make-up
8–12a	Blocking out and reading	Omit	Reading with script	Rehearse *without* script	First in pantomime only. Then with lines.	Dress rehearsal
12b–19a	Ditto	Reading with script	Omit	Ditto	Ditto	Dress rehearsal
19b–23	Ditto	Ditto	Rehearse *without* script	Ditto	Ditto	Dress rehearsal
CREW REPORTS FROM	Stage Manager, Electrician	3 Character sketches, costumes, props, publicity	3 Character sketches, make-up, bus. mgr.	Lights, costumes, make-up	All	All

FIGURE 2

the actors come to sense its onward movement toward the climax and resolution.

Moreover, when the director's criticisms are made, he should phrase them as much as he can in terms of meaning rather than in terms of "Do this" or "Don't do that." Above all, he should avoid forcing his own tricks of interpretation upon his actors. He should rather suggest the proper moods to them and help them to work out the interpretation which is most natural to themselves. Good acting flows outward from the actor's own imagination.

Let it be supposed that George and Harry are at stage center carrying on a conversation. George is facing Harry squarely so that his face is seen only in profile and, as a consequence, his words are not coming out into the auditorium so that they can be heard distinctly. Instead of saying, "George, face more front," the director will ask, "George, to whom are you really speaking those lines?" George's first impulse will be to say, "Why, to Harry, of course." However, in a moment he will probably see the point and say, "To the audience." Then, of his own accord, he will stand so that while he speaks to Harry the audience can hear every word. He will have become conscious of his audience and will speak primarily to them while continuing his simulated conversation with Harry. Instead of obeying a specific command referring to a single detail of his performance, he has become conscious of a basic principle of all good acting.

So with the correction of matters of interpretation. George has just been given very sad news yet continues to stand with the easy, confident carriage of his natural, youthful self. The wise director will not say, "George, slump your shoulders and let your head drop." Rather, he will ask questions such as, "George, how do you stand when you are feeling happy and confident? What happens to your muscles when you are sad? What does the information which Harry has just given you mean to you? Does it make you happy or sad?"

The director should not try to accomplish more at the first rehearsals than the mere blocking out of the stage positions and movements and the establishment of bits of business. True acting cannot so much as begin while the actor is bothered by his script. But just so soon as possible after this preliminary work is over, a date should be set when the actors must know their lines. From that date on the director should allow no manuscripts upon the stage. The actor should be made to depend upon the prompter if he cannot remember. The order of emphasis at successive rehearsals has already been indicated in the rehearsal schedules: first, convincing characterizations and clear vocal effects; second, the heightening of all conflicts; third, quickness in picking up cues and the importance of group playing; fourth, smoothness and continuity and the proper regulation of the tempo of the play.

The last few rehearsals of a play should be allowed to proceed with no interruptions whatever. The director should reserve all criticism until the end of the rehearsal. The final rehearsal will, of course, be in full costume and make-up with curtains operated and all lighting, scenic and sound effects exactly as they will be at the public performance. If the play has elaborate scenery or lighting, it will be well to hold separate scene and light rehearsals wherein the persons responsible can practise clearing the stage and setting it or operating the lights upon the proper cues. Nothing should be left to chance.

COMMON FAULTS

Here is a list of a few common faults which every director will find himself called upon to remedy:

(a) Lack of proper enunciation. This usually comes because of the failure of the amateur to pronounce his final consonants, especially his D's, T's, G's, and P's. These are not stressed in ordinary conversation, but upon the stage a player must stress them if he is to make them heard in the rear of the auditorium. Vowel-sounds naturally carry farther than consonants. The actor, must, therefore, stress the consonants—especially the final ones—if he is to make them carry as far as the vowels.

(b) Dropping the voice toward the end of the sentence. Many amateurs do this and it results in the audience losing that part of the sentence. It also gives the impression of a lack of vitality or vigor on the part of the actor.

(c) The lack of pause. All too often the amateur delivers a long speech without reference to punctuation marks and with only such pauses as he needs for taking breath. Usually the thought could be better expressed by a significant pause than by a continuous rush of words. In addition there should be "the fractional dash before a word or phrase which requires effective pointing."

(d) Awkwardness of hands. The director cannot legally amputate the hands of an actor when they continually obtrude in the interpretation of a part. He must, therefore, patiently labor until some natural way is found for the player to be using his hands. The director will not be continually calling attention to the player's hands, however, or to his feet, or to any other part of his anatomy, for this would only produce self-consciousness and more awkwardness. Rather the director's task is to help the actor to intensify his mental assimilation of his part so that he will want to use his hands to help express the mental attitude.

(e) Slow cues. Amateurs tend to let a sentence die away before taking up their cues. This slows the action of the play. Quick cues are essential to swift movement.

(f) Dropping out of character between speeches. Inexperienced actors are apt to cease acting in the intervals between their speeches, becoming their own natural selves with the mere addition of make-up and costume. They need to be reminded that every movement made upon the stage, or every failure to move, every bodily set or facial expression, should at all times be helping to tell a story to the audience. There should, of course, be no needless, attention-distracting movements on the part of the silent actor while another actor is speaking. But there should be some reaction to the other actor's speech portrayed, if it be only the intent attitude of listening. Good acting is a composite art of the entire stage group working toward one unified effect quite as much as it is a matter of an individual's delivery of his own lines.

THE NIGHT OF THE PRODUCTION

And now at last comes the night of production. The audience is assembled in front of the curtain, the players behind it. There is a moment of absolute quiet as the players gather around the director, all in costume and ready for their parts. It is a moment of suppressed excitement. Each player is probably thinking of himself, but he needs to forget himself and think of the message of the play and how to make it effective with the audience out front. So now the players bow their heads for a prayer, preferably from one or two members of the group as well as from the director, a prayer to unite them all in spirit and purpose, a prayer to bring peace and perspective to anxious minds. After the prayer, each player goes to his appointed place, the director out front. There will be an introductory service of music and reading to prepare the audience emotionally for the play. When it is finished the lights go out. There is a hushed moment, the curtain opens, and the play begins!

CHECK LIST FOR DIRECTOR

1. Have you helped your drama group to choose a play that meets the twelve tests of religious drama?
2. Have you organized a crew including: Business Manager, Publicity Manager, Stage Manager, Electrician, Costumer, Property Man, Make-Up Committee?
3. Have you provided each member of the crew and cast with a check list of his responsibilities and required regular reports of progress?
4. Have you insisted that all crew work be completed one week before the first public production?
5. Have you blocked out the play yourself before beginning rehearsals?
6. Have you made out a rehearsal schedule for your cast, indicating the dates and the particular emphases of each rehearsal?
7. Have you adhered faithfully to this rehearsal schedule?
8. Have you helped the individual players to overcome the common faults of: Poor enunciation, Dropping voice at end of sentences, Lack of pause, Slow cues, Awkwardness of hands, Failure to respond?
9. Have you achieved satisfactorily these fundamentals: Characterization, Composition, Picturization, Movement, Rhythm, Tempo (or Pacing), Pantomime, Religious effect?
10. Have you been on hand promptly at all rehearsals?
11. Have you kept the cast and crew working harmoniously so that they have had a sense of fellowship in creative accomplishment?
12. Have you planned and timed and rehearsed the enveloping service of worship so that it builds up the emotional foundation for the play and helps to produce the desired religious effect?

Chapter V

ACTING

SHALL the technique of acting in religious drama be learned from Hollywood, or from the legitimate theatre, or from those who have been struggling with the art before church congregations? Obviously the answer is, From all three, and from every other source that can shed any light upon it. But since the religious effect is the goal, and the religious spirit of the players must be the starting point, it may be well to begin with the experience of amateur church players, and then add to it and refine it with the discipline of those who have been working on stage and screen.

The ghosts of players in many a church production pass in review. Each one comes out of the mists of memory, pauses to tell what he learned in this or that play, and passes on into the blessed mists again. Listen to a few of them.

A FIRST EXPERIENCE

Here is a young man, who had his first acting experience in Mary Carolyn Davies' allegory, *A Slave with Two Faces*. He played the part of *Life*.

I came upon the stage innocent and expectant, with no previous performances to regret or cherish. In fact I was quite unaware of the whole process of acting. My first reaction was that things are not what they seem. I had watched people practise for a play and thought the exercise stupid. I had observed professional performances and had delighted in the results. But to read a line, have someone suggest the possible posture and then undertake the interpretation of that line seemed utterly impossible to me, and equally absurd to those who watched me try to do it.

My next significant discovery was that I must really feel what I was attempting to do, if it was to be the least bit effective. In fact, it was much easier to act if I thoroughly understood the meaning of the lines, thought about them apart from the acting, and then combined all three in an attempt to live as a slave or as a tyrant. No doubt the audiences were far from aware that such a process happened, but I felt it at times and deeply regretted I was not able always to feel it while on the stage.

Among my other discoveries as a pioneer explorer was the fact that it took an abundance of self-control to act. As an observer I noted the ease and poise of the actors, never thinking that they practised to attain it. I was troubled with my own awkwardness and inability to do what I knew should be done and what seemed quite simple to do. . . . The full significance and worth of the play came only after hard labor and much toiling.

There are a million details in acting that must be considered or the audience will not grasp the great idea, the climax will not come, and the proper interpretation of the playwright's work will not have been realized. Chief among these significant details would come: distinct articulation, smooth business, correct tempo, and an appropriate spirit within every member of the cast.

One never knows how stupid he is until he learns something. I have learned just enough to know that there is much to learn about acting, and I shall witness future plays with keener appreciation and greater admiration for those who have discovered so many of the secrets of acting.

"THE PLAY'S THE THING"

And here is a woman who played the part of *Judith* in Mary Hamlin's *He Came Seeing*.

The most fundamental thing I got out of this experience is a deeper realization of the truth that "The play's the thing," and everything must be subordinate to that fact. Every member of the cast must have the same conception of what the play means and how to express it; and since naturally each one would have an individual, and therefore different, conception, the only way to attain unity is for each to try to understand and adopt for his own the interpretation of the director, and forget his own individual one. This fundamental conception of the meaning of the play and the manner of its presentation, I learned, must underlie all else, and be the spring of interpretation on the part of the actors.

I learned as I never have as an auditor or spectator, that the play had a very definite rhythm, growing out of a fundamental conception of the director and cast, and that this rhythm will determine many things, or require many things, about the play: its tempo, its intensity, the balance of its parts. In so far as any character failed in grasping the fundamental conception of the play, he failed to feel this rhythm, and he was, therefore, a discord in the play. I feel sure there were times when I was the discord in the play, because my own reactions are swift and intense and ran away with me, getting me out of tempo.

The principal thing I learned for myself is that feeling, however genuine and sincere, is not enough, but needs behind it a sure grasp of the artistry required to express emotion, and the means of controlling and presenting it. My own main difficulty was that I was constantly losing myself in the situation, and finding myself so tense and so breathless that when the time came for me to speak I did not have myself in hand to deliver my lines. I know that the artist does not do that—he has always the necessary control to do what he has to do not only with feeling but with discrimination, and he has himself and gives the audience a sense of reserve behind his self-control. I was a very great sinner here, but I found it very very hard to keep in character at all if I tried to reduce my intensity. Not only did my failure make it impossible for me to keep the situation in hand, but it must have spoiled the rhythm of the play and unbalanced the other players. For of course another essential of the truth that "the play's the thing" is that each character must keep himself strictly subordinate to the play as a whole—he must adequately fill his part certainly, but to overact it destroys the balance as truly as to be inadequate.

SOME A. B. C.'S

Following her comes the young man who played *Joab*, her son, in the same play.

Among the first things I learned in *He Came Seeing* was the fact that by having my lines fairly well in mind by the first rehearsal, I could lend myself more freely to interpretation and action. Before actually learning the speeches themselves I made myself familiar with the meaning of each line or group of lines to be spoken while I was upon the stage. Then having the general trend of each speech and the episodes in mind, I learned my lines together with my cues. After learning my lines I frequently sat down and read the play as written to make myself more certain of the actual text. Often while driving to or from school I repeated my part from memory.

Far more difficult for me than learning lines was the problem of ridding my voice of its monotony, due to frequent falling inflections. In part I was able to do this, but only with practise, and then not even to my own satisfaction.

While my gestures were not always correct or graceful, I

found that gesture itself, as well as all stage movement and action, came very natural to me when I felt my part.

Joab has an unusually fine opportunity for character development in the course of the play, and for that reason was a very interesting part to play. Of all the parts available, I could not have hoped to find a part I would enjoy more.

Each episode must build up to its own climax and end with a meaningful picture, if the play is to move on to a fitting final climax, which makes the play convincing.

The spirit of each member of the cast, as well as the spirit of the cast as a whole, affects each member of the cast both directly and indirectly. The moment of prayerful meditation before the producing had a quieting and uplifting effect upon me.

CO-OPERATION AND CONSECRATION

Now comes a stalwart man, mature yet still young, who had the difficult rôle of Kruger in *The Great Choice*.

Though I had not been so simple as to believe "that where two or three are gathered together it is time to put on a play," I had not quite sensed the combination of science and art and hard work to produce effectively a play.

The first principle that came upon me with a new emphasis in the production of this play was the importance of co-operation and helping one another. There were times when I was tempted to criticize my fellow participants, and then with a backward look I often discovered that I had not so acted my part as to give them a chance or reason for doing their part in the best manner. Time and again I felt that some individual was not coming through with his part as he should, only to discover that I had not made it possible for him or her so to do. This is so evident now as one looks back over the evolution of the production through the rehearsals. We all started out with a hazy idea of the parts we were to portray. As we practised there would dawn upon one or another of us a new or fuller interpretation; this would in turn inspire a new and fuller interpretation in another character, so the production evolved, each player depending upon the others, and being helped and hindered by them whether he would or not.

The technique of building up the emotional responses and reaching a climax in each episode and following in the next episode a little lower than the climax of the preceding one, and going a little higher and so on to the final climax of the play, I found to be a difficult one to master. Indeed, I have not mastered it, but I feel that I do sense the need and wisdom of it now as I had not done before. I also appreciate its difficulty more than I have heretofore. On paper it looked quite easy, but in practise it is a different matter. I found it rather difficult not to let the emotional tone rather completely subside after each episode. Following this consideration there naturally comes that of the tempo and rhythm of the movement. As we came along near the end of our preparation, I began to feel a very definite rhythm which was in both productions more pronounced to me than in any of our rehearsals.

Neither had I before quite realized the full import of magnifying action on the stage. The need of not only acting the part of the character being portrayed, but magnifying that action for the benefit of the audience, came to me in this production with greater clarity and force. Closely related to this point, but not quite identical, is that of the gestures being full and clearly cut so they may be fully seen and comprehended by all of the audience.

In rather close connection with such considerations comes the greater use to be made of the pause. The need of clear pronunciation and enunciation, and the carrying of the final syllables of a sentence out so they are not lost, all were brought to my attention.

In a religious drama, particularly, the value of a spiritual consecration cannot be over emphasized. Perhaps the practise of such prayerful consecration just before a production is of greater value in our group than it would be with a younger or more diversified group in a church. It was of great significance to me, and I cannot but believe it would be in any group. Certainly it is one of the logical times for prayer.

Next comes a thoughtful and serious-minded youth, who found a religious experience in acting the title rôle of Edna Baldwin's *Ba Thane*.

One of the criteria for religious drama in the Church is the effect which it has on the players themselves. It is a way of learning by doing. Gradually and almost unconsciously the player seems to undergo a leavening process, in which the yeast of "spiritual values" helps him to rise expansively into a larger experience of insight and interpretation. In short, he is helped to rise above himself. And while there is a deliberate striving toward the learning of lines and the portrayal of character on the stage, it is hard to escape the involuntary assimilation of those deeper values which lie below the level of conscious endeavor. They seem to be resting there, only waiting to be awakened from their slumber. There is a price to pay in acting, but there is also a compensation to be received. And the compensation need not be confined merely to the experience of living itself. This, I believe, is the "saving grace" of true religious drama. And this is my own personal reaction to playing the part of Ba Thane. I have "learned" something from the experience.

In trying to portray Ba Thane as the person he would be in actual life, I was impressed anew with the joy of using one's imagination creatively. He seemed to be a big bundle of "57 varieties"! At first it was not exactly enjoyable, this thing of trying to achieve the proper shades and contrasts in moods, particularly when so much of Ba Thane's character was not natural to me. But the more I read and re-read the lines, the more was I gripped by mental images as to how Ba Thane would act if he were there himself. But he wasn't there, and wasn't going to be there! Very well, I would simply put my own soul into the situation and do my best to take his place. Right there the joy began! It was the joy of getting out of myself and into Ba Thane—something as a prisoner must feel when he is released. Ba Thane was an exceedingly stimulating fellow, interesting to study and admire. He said to me: "You can't even begin to fill my place unless you begin to use your own imagination." And while it seems to me that I filled his place rather feebly, I am glad for the possibilities he showed me in the use of the whole body—hands, feet, face, eyes and mouth—for the expression of mental images.

It is one thing to read plays and discuss the elements of dramatic interest from a book; and it is another thing to experience the application of these elements. I was much impressed with the way in which these elements, as we discussed them in class and analyzed them in plays read, measured up in this play. It seemed that practically every one was present, and served a real part in dramatic appeal. The character-revelation was good, and the contrasting moods were strong. Though the episodic structure was somewhat heavy, the total effect was at least in the direction of unity and completeness. Certainly there was present a good deal of the emotional, the conflict of wills, and the choice of action. The solution was essential and natural; the climax came at high altitude, and I am sure the audience must have felt the suspense.

Obviously, we who are interested in religious drama are eager to help others on the road to richer experiences through the dwelling of the mind on things worth while. And if we can catch the significance of those necessary elements of dramatic interest, which help to carry some great meaning into the lives of an audience, then shall we not have profited much by taking part as actors ourselves?

EMOTIONAL CONTROL AND TEAM WORK

The girl who interpreted Mademoiselle Rose in François Coppée's *The Lord's Prayer,* learned the relation of control of the emotions to the control of the voice and body. She says:

One of the most important things I learned was the importance of proper pronunciation. Acting in this play helped train my ear. Having been accustomed to provincialisms all my life I was not conscious of using them. Even when I learned what was right I could not always be sure whether I had or had not dropped back into bad habits of speech. All of the actors in our group seemed to have provincial speech habits. Hearing the others criticized and learning to tell the difference in them made me more conscious of my own.

Another important thing which I learned was the value of team work in the play as a whole. At the beginning we seemed to be separate units moving around performing our parts. There was no give and take, no response because of the emotion of a fellow actor. Since the curé and I had the longest and most difficult part together, we practised together more. We could actually begin to see where a sympathetic response arose between the two characters. One of us would say in rehearsal, "I'm not getting that with you." Or, on the other hand, at the end of the last two or three rehearsals we felt a sort of real satisfaction that we finally had got into the spirit of the thing together.

I learned, too, the importance of controlled emotion and its relation to control of voice and body. The beginning of this control is in breathing from the diaphragm. The most important step in the process is the relaxation of throat. Before going on the stage I practised an exercise for complete relaxation, and consciously sought for relaxation of the throat. An open throat thoroughly relaxed prevents loss of control of emotions. When the throat is tense the voice gets harsher and shriller and the audience gets the effect of more or less hysterical emotion. Deep breathing has a soothing and calming effect which nothing else can have. All this tends to produce good voice, which is as important a factor in acting as there is.

I learned that players must adjust emotions and their expressions to those of fellow players. My voice was too strong and my actions too forceful to tone in well with the others. No play can be successful unless the players learn to adjust to make a harmonious whole.

The value to an actor of good direction is very important. When good business was suggested we found ourselves getting into the swing of the action much more naturally. Someone standing off could view the whole effect and see our faults much better than we could ever hope to do. One could learn his awkward mannerisms, slouches, etc. As in the case of the provincialisms of pronunciation we had awkward postures, gestures, etc., of which we were unconscious. As nobody hesitated to point them out one soon became painfully aware of them. I shall forever after watch my feet positions.

Best of all was the real spirit of helpfulness exhibited by everybody—the cheerfulness and kindliness back of all the banter; the really genuine spirit of comradeship which is after all the result to be gained by giving religious plays whether one is actor, stage-manager, director, or general flunkey.

MAKING THE CHARACTER REAL

Finally, in this procession of players of religious drama comes a young man who found a stirring adventure in the exploration of a character. He relates it:

The opening of the fall quarter of school found me in a peculiarly anxious, depressed state of mind. A flood of the uncertain minutiæ of living had succeeded in drowning out of my consciousness the zestful wonder of life itself.

Then came my attempt to interpret the rôle of Uncle Toby, the joyous mender of clocks and healer of sick souls in the play *The Tinker*. Uncle Toby was a modern incarnation of the spirit which had lived in St. Francis of Assisi. I read two standard lives of the saint and lived in daily thought of him trying to capture the proper spirit of the rôle. It was hard to rise to the spiritual atmosphere of a Francis, but what a wonderful experience when at last it came! Really to see and feel life through the character of one who had dared make the adventure of complete trust in its goodness, who had sloughed off all its petty cares in a glorious self-forgetfulness—this was to find a veritable spiritual resurrection.

DEVELOPING THE ART

To the findings of these amateur adventurers in religious drama can be added the more mature suggestions and observations of those who have worked long in the theatre. The wisest and ablest among them will be the first to recognize that these neophytes have already discovered for themselves some of the basic principles of acting. And they will be first to agree that without the eager spirit and humble devotion of these young players, all the tricks of the professional actor will be but sounding brass and clanging cymbal.

But granted this, these novices have only begun, only suggested, the first steps of the art of interpreting character. How shall the actor who has the cooperative spirit and the teachable mind go about it to acquire further skill? Let him begin by becoming intimately acquainted with the character he is to portray. This takes time and patient effort. It will involve the search for similar characters in actual life and the observation of them, noting their dress and personal appearance, the way they think and how they feel, their facial expressions, their gestures, and all their distinctive mannerisms. The actor will also delve into his own store of life experiences in the attempt to find situations somewhat analogous to those in which the character is placed. From this he will gain some clue to the character's emotional state. Often the actor will profit by reading biographies of persons who have lived lives similar to that of the character. Especially in the case of an actual historic personage will the actor want to read as many biographies as he can find. Moreover, if the play is laid in some day other than the actor's own, he will want to make himself acquainted with its happenings, its manners, and its ways of thinking. True character creation always goes far beyond a mere study of the lines of the play.

Once thus intimately acquainted with the character he is to portray, the actor's next problem centers about this question, "How can I make this character live in the inner experience of the men and women in the audience?" This brings us to the statement of the basic principle upon which all good acting, considered as an objective art, is based—the principle of empathy.

BRINGING THE AUDIENCE INTO THE PLAY

If we see a child tottering on the edge of a cliff, invariably our own muscles tense and we find *ourselves making the very motions that we wish he would make to save himself.* And immediately this happens we feel within ourselves the emotion of terror. Why? First, because man is by nature imitative. Second, man's emotional states are very definitely related to the state of his physical self—to its glandular activity and its muscular tensions. Because of this there is for every human emotion a characteristic bodily attitude or movement which, observing in another, we tend to imitate, and thereby come to feel the emotion within ourselves. This imitative road to the stirring up of emotion is known in the psychology of acting as the principle of empathy (literally, to feel into).

The good actor, knowing that it is his primary job to arouse emotional appreciation of the play, will consciously take advantage of this principle. In his acting he will give the audience the physical *cue which will call forth their empathic response and so lead them actually to feel into the play. This means that the actor will act with his whole body.* But he need not make the complete series of motions which he would make in a corresponding real-life situation. In fact it is as he *restrains* himself and only *suggests* a motion that the audience is led to the greatest intensity of desire to make it *for him* and so comes to feel the emotion itself most keenly.

WHERE IDENTIFICATION STOPS AND ART BEGINS

Identification of the actor with his character is good up to a certain point. That point is determined by the principle known as aesthetic balance. In brief this implies two things for the actor:

First, he must never establish direct communication with the audience either by looking into their faces or by directing his speeches straight to them. This would destroy the aesthetic distance which allows them to view the play pleasurably as more or less of a dream vision rather than reality.

Second, he must never so lose himself in his rôle that

his real self is no longer master but is actually held and swayed by the emotional storms of the character he is portraying. The true actor, for all his sympathetic understanding of his character and a large amount of genuine feeling of his part, must yet preserve his distance from the rôle and be at all times the artist who is master of the effect he produces.

MAKING EVERY MOVEMENT HELP TO TELL THE STORY

The audience has come with the desire to have a story told to it. Everything which helps give the audience this story is good. Everything which distracts attention to something else is bad. Therefore let every action be clearly motivated. Aimless, puttering movements which tell no story other than the actor's own nervousness should be eliminated.

Let the actor be careful how he crosses the stage with reference to other actors who may be upon it. All movement attracts attention to the moving object. Therefore the actor will seldom if ever cross the stage while another actor is speaking unless the immediate action of the play requires it. The center of the story's interest belongs to the actor who is delivering the lines. When a line requires a cross during its delivery, the actor may cross either before or behind a fellow actor, usually behind. In the interest both of grace of movement and of stage balance, the actor who is being crossed should, as a general rule, take a few steps in the opposite direction while the actor who is making the cross passes by him. The question of whether to cross in front or behind is to be determined by whichever cross happens to be the least bothersome to the audience.

THE IMPORTANCE OF PANTOMIME

Pantomime, as Madame Eva Alberti says in her *Handbook of Acting,* is the "moving, vibrating part of the play." She defines pantomime as "the expression of thoughts and emotions through bodily action." Since the audience *sees* a play as well as *hears* it, it follows that this bodily action must express the same thoughts and emotions as the actor's words. Here the novice often comes to grief. His words say, "You shall not pass!" while his bodily movements say, "What's the use?" or "How weary and tubercular I am!" To discipline her own students in pantomimic expression Madame Alberti puts them through a series of exercises such as the following:

Imagine you hear and react to:
An explosion near by; then far away.
Someone screaming in the next room.
A loud crash of thunder.
A favorite tune.
A friend's voice.

Imagine you see and react to:
A flash of lightning.
A rose; a violet; a daisy.
A friend; someone you dislike.
A child; a horse; a cat; a dog.

Imagine you taste and react to:
Lemon.
Candy.

Let the actor put himself through a series of such exercises of his own invention, or those in her book, and he will gradually acquire the ability to express with his body the emotions and thoughts of his heart. A severe but excellent test for any scene is to have the players go through it entirely in pantomime and without words. Unless the story, thus silently told, gets across in its main outlines to a stranger in the rear row there is something inadequate about the pantomime.

POSITION AND GROUPING

Because the men and women in front of the curtain wish at all times to read the changing expressions upon the player's face, let him turn away from them as little as possible. In a conversation between two characters they should seldom face each other squarely so that their faces are seen only in profile. Rather, lines drawn across the toes of each instead of being parallel will meet to form a $\wedge$ with its apex pointing upstage. This will bring each actor facing half toward his audience and half toward his fellow. This would, of course, apply also to the position of their chairs if seated.

A group of several characters in conversation will distribute its members so that the actor with the most important lines to deliver will be upstage from the others at the apex of a roughly triangular grouping. Then his face will always be toward the audience. Likewise, if two characters are seated upon a bench which stands at an angle to the audience rather than parallel to it, the more important character will be seated at the upstage end of the bench.

THE PICTURE-FRAME STAGE AND THE ACTOR

The stage as seen by the audience is much like a picture framed by the proscenium arch. Not only must the entire stage be set but the actors themselves grouped upon it with due regard for the principles of good pictorial composition. Players must not crowd to one side or the other but rather distribute themselves so as to maintain balance. Moreover, since stage center is the focal point of the audience's interest, all important action will tend toward that spot.

Further, an actor's movements will be influenced by the grace of their appearance as viewed through the frame of the proscenium. Thus, if an actor stands facing one side or the other of the stage, he will have his upstage rather than his downstage foot advanced. In this position, if he gestures, he will gesture with his upstage arm. And should he drop upon one knee, his weight will rest upon the knee downstage while the upstage foot will be advanced.

For a complete discussion of the technique of stage movement and grouping, the reader is referred to the standard books listed in the bibliography. Only a few obvious points remain to be mentioned to complete the more elementary discussion at which this manual aims. Since, if the work of the lighting artist has been well done, the stage will seldom be illuminated in all its portions with equal intensity, the actor should avoid shadowed areas when giving lines whose accompanying facial expressions are important. Actors will also distribute themselves so as to avoid crowding. Every actor needs freedom for gesture and movement. And, lastly, he will try to avoid hiding his fellows from the view of the audience by playing in front of them. If, however, an actor at the rear or side of the stage finds that he cannot see the audience, it is a safe assumption that neither can the audience see him. He should then quietly take a step or so to one side or the other until the defect is remedied.

All of these matters of stage position and movement are, primarily, the responsibility of the director. This should be clearly understood. Yet every good actor should understand the principles involved in order that he may obey the director's commands with intelligence.

THAT OLD GENTLEMAN IN THE REAR

But it is not only important that the audience see the play. They must hear it as well. It will help the amateur actor if he will keep continually before his mind's eye the vision of a fine old gentleman with failing hearing who came a bit late and had to take a seat in the farthest row in the rear of the auditorium. That old gentleman is leaning forward in his eagerness to hear every word that is spoken. It is the actor's duty to make his enunciation so distinct and to give such volume to his voice that that old gentleman will truly enjoy the play.

If the actor would have a voice with carrying power and one responsive to every emotional shading of his interpretation, let him learn to do these four things: first, to breathe easily and deeply from the diaphragm, not from the upper chest; second, to keep a relaxed throat; third, to form the words well forward upon the tongue rather than back in the throat, and, fourth, to use his lips as well as his voice.

Mere carrying power alone will not suffice to make that old gentleman understand. The actor's words must be well clipped apart. He must also take especial care to pronounce his final consonants. And he must avoid the common fault of dropping his voice at the close of a speech, as if the last words were not quite as important as the first.

Distinct enunciation is a matter of opening the mouth

and making free use of lips and tongue and teeth in forming the words. The actor will profit much by standing in front of his mirror while repeating with exaggerated lip and jaw and tongue movements such a tongue twister as the familiar "Peter Piper picked a peck of pickled peppers." Then while still before the mirror, let him repeat his lines with the same exaggerated muscular movements.

HOW TO MEMORIZE LINES

Good acting cannot so much as begin until lines are thoroughly mastered. The method used in memorizing is of prime importance. Let the player first read over the entire play several times to fix the movement of the plot in his mind and to come to see his own part in relation to the play as a whole. Then let him go back and work upon memorization episode by episode, rather than page by page, reading the speeches of the other actors as well as his own and paying especial attention to the last sentence of each speech immediately preceding one of his own—his cue for speaking. Let him do this work of memorization upon his feet, walking through the accompanying action and reading his speeches aloud. Later, when he believes himself to be letter perfect, he can have someone read his cues to him and test his ability to reply. This method fixes the words in the actor's mind through a whole series of associations—visual, motor, and auditory, as well as those which belong to the entire flow of the play's movement and meaning.

PUTTING LIFE INTO THE LINES

There are three simple practises which are of high value to the actor in thinking himself into his part: First, let him go through his script pencil in hand and in every speech underline the important word or words. Second, let him make marginal notes in his script to indicate the mood and tempo of all his speeches and the modulations of intensity which mark the emotional flow of every episode. Third, let the actor indulge in no off-stage conversations between the opening of the play and the final curtain. Let him do nothing while off-stage to break character, but rather spend his time quietly waiting, with his mind intent upon the progress of events that are supposed to be taking place in the part of the character he is portraying. Then he will be prepared both in mood and thought for his next entrance.

Most amateur plays suffer from the monotony of the actor's delivery. The artificial monstrosities of the old declamatory style of acting belong forever to the past. Yet the player will do well to take advantage of every legitimate opportunity his lines afford him to vary the tempo of his delivery and the pitch, volume, and intensity of his voice according to meaning and emotional stress.

In this connection let the player remember that often *a significant pause has a greater emotional value than a continuous flow of words*. There are times when our emotions master us too deeply for fluent speech. The pause may also be effectively used as a fractional dash employed before an important word to center attention and to give emphasis to what follows.

The sum of this whole matter of interpretation of lines may be stated as follows: First, all of the character's speeches should be so delivered that their every shade of meaning and emotion is made both clear and compelling. Second, the interest of the audience should never be lost through monotony but continually brought back and freshened by skilful yet natural and appropriate variations of the tempo, pitch, and volume of delivery. And third, the whole effect should be so spontaneous and fresh that the audience will forget that the actor is repeating memorized lines and be held under the illusion that every line is being spoken for the first time in response to the situation which calls it forth.

PROMPTNESS ON CUES AND ENTRANCE

Individual lines may be delivered with admirable skill and the play yet drag unless cues are picked up quickly. The actor will, of course, avoid such speed in picking up his cues as will give the effect of stepping upon the other actor's lines. He will, however, learn to anticipate the exact moment when his speech should begin and be ready. In the case of broken speeches let the actor responsible for the interruption find his impulse for speaking a word or so in advance of the exact spot at which he is to interrupt. *But let every actor with a broken speech always have a complete sentence in his mind which he can complete should the second actor fail to interrupt him properly.* Nothing is more painful than a broken speech dangling in the air waiting to be interrupted.

Of equal or even greater importance than the prompt picking up of cues is the matter of prompt entrances. A delayed entrance holds up the entire flow of speech and action upon the stage. No worthy actor will fail his responsibility for making every entrance at the exact moment it should be made, neither sooner nor later. If he does fail he will merit the castigation if not the violence of his fellow players.

POINTING THE CLIMAXES

A play which stays upon the same level of emotional intensity from beginning to end is a play that has failed. Every play is made up of a series of episodes, each one of which rises to a climax somewhere near its close and then shades off into the opening of the succeeding episode. These emotional peaks will vary in height. In general, each one will rise a bit higher than the one preceding it and all will sweep onward toward the climax of the play as a whole. Needless to say, this final climax should over-top all of the lesser climaxes of the episodes which have prepared the way for it.

The actor will aid this climactic movement of the play by playing the opening of each episode more lightly, increasing his intensity as the climax approaches. At the opening of an episode he will allow considerable space between himself and the other actors upon the stage, closing this distance up gradually as the episode gains in intensity. Especially will he close up the distance between himself and that character or group of characters with whom he is in conflict as the episode nears its climax. The whole principle may be illustrated by the typical fight between two small boys which opens with the participants on opposite sides of the street calling each other names and closes with the exchange of blows.

THAT VITAL TEAMWORK

Nor can a play succeed if each actor stands out as an individual. A play is an artistic whole. Its successful production requires teamwork and group playing on the part of all the actors. There is no room for "star parts." Nor should the actor ever be tempted to underestimate the importance of the minor part in making toward the success of the whole. Throughout every phase of his preparation there should run a painstaking regard for each detail for it is details that make or mar the performance.

THE ACTOR'S ETHICS

On this subject a player once wrote from a background of hardly won personal conviction:

Individualism is a luxury which an actor cannot afford; not because it is immoral, but because it is inexpedient and, in the end, self-defeating. Highest efficiency in concerted action demands an ideal which will enshrine the success of the approaching production as the absolute standard for all matters of private conduct.

The individual should do nothing to interfere with his personal efficiency, such as going to bed at 2:00 a.m. the night before, or eating a heavy meal or talking himself hoarse before the production.

He should feel duty bound to create or reinforce the hopefulness and enthusiasm of the group, refraining from cynical comments or dismal forecasts, though such a self-imposed censorship is only a temporary measure to preserve the morale of the army, and may be removed immediately upon the cessation of hostilities at the end of the performance.

The individual should sacrifice both private comfort and the privilege of yielding to melancholy or any other temperamental mood in order to contribute the more effectively to the mechanical details of staging the play and to the group spirit.

Every director will breathe a fervent "amen" to that! And he will probably add at least two further points of ethics: (1) an actor should always arrive promptly at every rehearsal, for his delay wastes the time of the entire cast and spoils the morale of the group; (2) He should have his lines memorized by the time set by the director, for failure or slowness here holds back the group.

Summing up now the major factors that distinguish a competent actor from a careless one, and placing them in parallel columns for contrast, we have the following:

EARMARKS

OF A COMPETENT ACTOR

OF A CARELESS ACTOR

1. Anticipates all of his speeches and is ready to deliver them convincingly at exactly the right moment. Never relaxes his responsibility for making every entrance at the precise instant when it should be made—neither too soon, so as to interrupt the preceding episode, nor too late, so as to hold up the entire flow of action upon the stage.

1. Slow on cues. Allows the play to drag while remembering it is his turn to speak. Likewise careless in timing his entrances, thereby repeatedly holding up the entire action of the play.

2. Studies his lines by the whole method, episode by episode, on his feet, reading them aloud with appropriate expression and accompanying movement and business. Is letter perfect early in the course of rehearsals and does not require prompting.

2. Never sure of his lines. Stumbles over words and has to be prompted.

3. Speaks his lines so as to bring out their full meaning and emotional content. Makes a discriminating use of the pause for the expression of emotion and also for concentrating attention upon following important words or phrases. So varies his speeches in tempo, pitch and volume as to hold and freshen interest continually. Gives all speeches with such freshness and spontaneity that the audience forgets that they are memorized and believes they are being given for the first time.

4. Knows his character thoroughly and never drops out of character a single instant while on the stage, whether speaking or listening, in action or repose. Moreover, he remains in character while off-stage awaiting an entrance, keeping his mind intent upon the events supposed to be happening to the character, so that his next entrance is as completely convincing as was his last exit.

5. Makes his every movement or lack of movement

3. Speaks his lines as if the author had forgotten to put in any punctuation marks. Hurries through them as if it were a sin to make an effective and meaningful pause anywhere in the speech. Voice meanwhile stays on the same dead, expressionless level throughout the speech. No changes in quality or pitch of voice tones to indicate that the speaker is an emotional being who knows surprise, sorrow, fear, disgust, self-pity, optimism, sympathy, or any of the score of other human emotions.

4. Drops out of character when not speaking. Forgets that the set of his body, the changing expressions upon his face, his every movement or failure to move while upon the stage should be helping to tell a story to the audience, or stirring their emotions.

5. Fidgets about with aimless movements of hands

while upon the stage tell a story. Supplants all tendencies to nervous fidgeting by making his entire body an expressive instrument of his character portrayal, thus giving his audience the needed physical basis for their empathic response and causing them actually to share the emotional development of the play.

or feet or head. Forgets that unless an actor makes a movement with the purpose of telling a story to the audience he shouldn't move at all, minor shifts of position to preserve stage balance alone excepted, and these latter are, of course, purposeful.

6. Speaks with such volume and such distinctness of enunciation that his every word can be easily heard by the last man in the last row of seats in the auditorium.

6. Fails to speak loudly enough to be heard beyond the fifth row of seats. Fails to enunciate his words clearly. Drops the volume of his voice at the end of his lines, forgetting that the audience must hear the final word of a speech quite as well as the first.

7. Always on time at rehearsals. Indulges in no fits of temperament or any other practise which would interfere with his own efficiency as an actor or the efficiency of his fellows. Remembers that the message of the play as a whole is the thing of importance and strives to cooperate with the rest of the cast in perfect teamwork to the end of making that message emotionally compelling.

7. Is late to rehearsals. Indulges in fits of temperament. Fails to remember that convincing acting is as dependent upon teamwork as upon individual brilliance.

Chapter VI

BUSINESS MANAGEMENT

THE PRICE OF CARELESSNESS

A PLAY had been carefully worked up and had already been given a number of times with marked success. Then the business manager received a request to have the play produced before a small convention of religious workers meeting in one of Chicago's largest hotels. He promptly made arrangements by letter concerning the exact date and hour of the requested production and drew up a careful financial agreement to cover the expense involved. This done he rested upon the assurance that the secretary of the convention had given him that a stage would be provided and all details of the program cared for by the convention.

The night of the production came. An hour before time for the play to be given, the cast, loaded into an ancient five-passenger Ford belonging to one of the members and with a disreputable-appearing kitchen cupboard used in the play strapped upon the running board, drove up to the main entrance of the hotel and stopped to enquire where they should go. They were met by the outraged stare of the liveried doorman and told to "Get that thing out of there!" (referring, of course, to the car). There followed a lively altercation during which the doorman professed complete ignorance of any such religious gathering as was referred to and made it painfully clear that in all events the cast would neither bring their properties in at the main entrance nor leave their shabby car parked there. In the course of time the rear entrance to the hotel was located, the Ford safely parked, the convention room found, and the breathless players threaded their way to their proper destination through the labyrinthian ways of a large hotel, lugging their cupboard and suitcases with them.

But grief followed grief, for when the cast at last found their stage it proved to be an inadequate affair but poorly lighted, while for dressing rooms there was but one corner of the convention room curtained off. Within that curtained corner a mixed cast of men and women had to hastily devise such makeshift means as modesty demanded and robe themselves for the play. Small wonder that when, a half an hour late, the curtains at last parted upon the play itself the cast was almost hysterical and gave but a poor performance of a play in which they had previously won honor.

THE BUSINESS MANAGER'S PRIME QUALIFICATION

What was wrong? A mere trifle, but what a world of trouble it caused! The business manager had neglected to enquire concerning the exact type of stage offered, its lighting, the dressing room facilities available, the particular room in the hotel where the play was to be given, and the way to reach that room with the necessary stage properties. The prime qualification of a good business manager is the capacity for taking infinite pains with a large number of details.

To the casual glance the job of business manager for a play given by a church-drama group may appear to be relatively simple. So it is. Yet it involves painstaking care for a number of essential details by which the success of the play may be made or broken as surely as by the competence or incompetence of the director himself.

SECURING THE ENGAGEMENT

It is the business manager's duty to secure engagements for the cast. To this end he will first thoroughly familiarize himself with the play. He will be prepared to answer questions about its playing time, its theme, its story, its characters, etc.

Armed with this knowledge and knowing the exact dates upon which it is possible for the cast itself to produce the play, let the business manager go out to seek engagements. He will look about to find those churches, clubs, or other institutions most apt to be interested in the type of play he has to offer. He will secure personal interviews with the heads of these institutions. Should it happen that the players do not wish to produce the play in any other than their own church, let the business manager yet remember his responsibility for settling the time and place of the production. It is still his responsibility to interview the pastor of the church in regard to securing a place upon the church calendar of events.

There are a number of items which the business manager will make clear to the head of any institution engaging his play.

First, there must be an exact agreement as to the amount of money which is to be paid for the play's production. Next, in the case of a royalty play, the business manager must learn whether this sum is to be secured by charging admission or by taking a free will offering as this often affects the amount of royalty charged by the publishers.

Next comes the matter of programs. The business manager must learn whether he himself is to be responsible for the printing of the programs and advertising or whether the institution inviting the players will do this. In the latter instance the business manager will provide typewritten "copy" giving all the necessary items of information for the programs, including the name of the play, the division into acts or scenes, the cast, etc. Especially in the case of a royalty play will he see that due acknowledgment is made to the owner of the copyright. A sample program is given below.

A DRAMATIC SERVICE OF WORSHIP

Conducted by the Seminary Players under the direction of Dr. Fred Eastman.

Monday evening, January 25, at 8.30 o'clock.

Mr. Sam T. Lenters, presiding.
Professor Cecil M. Smith, organist.

Organ Prelude
Hymn No. 64, *O God, our Help in Ages Past.*
Responsive Reading, Selection number 61.
Hymn No. 351, *In Christ there is no East or West* (To *Dundee,* No. 90).
Prayer

A Religious Drama: *Ba Thane,* by Edna A. Baldwin.

The characters in the order of their appearance:

JOAN WORTH, *the daughter* . . . Mary Anderson
VIRGINIA WORTH, *the wife* . . . . Ruth Cooper
MA MAY, *a young Burmese girl* . . . Mary Dodge

GORDON WORTH, *an American missionary* Victor Schuldt
RICHARD ORDWAY, *an American newspaper*
    reporter . . . . Richard Hulbert
BA THANE, *Ma May's brother* . . Verdette Walters
JOE FOX, *an American oil-driller* . . Clarence Parr

The scene is laid in a missionary home in Burma. The time is five o'clock on a March evening.

Hymn No. 355, *Come, Kingdom of Our God.*

Benediction.

NOTES

The play, *Ba Thane,* was written in the Seminary's class in Drama Writing and is published by the Student Volunteer Movement. The author is a missionary to Burma.

The Congregation is requested not to applaud.

Had the above play been a royalty play, the program would have borne the following note:

This play is produced by special arrangement with (here would be inserted the name of the person or publishing house holding the copyright).

SECURING INFORMATION FOR DIRECTOR AND CAST

As already indicated the business manager must also secure exact information concerning the size, condition, and lighting arrangements of the stage upon which the play is to be given, also the dressing room facilities available. He will learn, too, the best route of travel for the players to take in going to fulfil their engagement. In doing so he will note the schedule of all train service which must be used and the amount of the fare to be paid. He will know these things surely and not depend upon information of the "I think" variety. In the case of the stage and its equipment he will see it for himself rather than depend upon another's description.

MANAGING THE FINANCES

The business manager is responsible for the finances of the play. To this end he will at the very beginning secure estimates of all probable expenses, consulting the costumer, stage manager, electrician, property manager, and make-up manager, and adding the royalty charges and cost of books. On this basis, and in consultation with the director, he will budget all expenditures and hold all members of the cast to this budget in their expenditure of funds. He will require each member of the cast who spends money upon the play to turn in an itemized and receipted bill for sums spent and will give out no money from the treasury of the organization apart from such itemized receipts. The business manager will keep an exact account of all sums received and expended and will make a complete report to the director the day after the production. A model of such a report follows:

REPORT OF THE BUSINESS MANAGER FOR
THE VALIANT

Number of productions	2
Receipts:	
Offering from the Hyde Park Congregational Church (January 28)	$16.40
Offering from the Auburn Park Congregational Church (February 24)	25.00
Total	$41.40

Expenditures:

Royalty on the January 28th performance .	$10.00
Royalty on the February 24th performance .	10.00
Electric light bulbs (January 8)	5.00
Other electrical supplies—batteries, plugs, etc. (January 10)	2.40
Priest's collar (January 15)	.20
Cambric (January 15)	.45
Tissue paper (January 15)	.15
Cosmetics (January 25)	1.35
Electric light sockets and double connections (February 20)	.45
Friction and binding tape (February 20) . .	.45
Car fare (February 24)	.50

Total . . .	$30.95

Total receipts to date .	$41.40
Total expenditures to date	30.95

On hand, February 25 .	$10.45

Receipted bills attached.
Signed,

J. A. JENKINS
Business Manager for *The Valiant*
The Seminary Players.

All royalties are payable in advance and should be paid in strict accord with the terms noted by the publisher of the play.

In cases where, at the close of a performance, the business manager is given the free will offering, he should make sure that the money has been counted before it is delivered into his possession and that the pastor or other church official giving it over knows the exact sum of it.

PREPARING THE HOUSE FOR THE PLAY

In addition to his other duties it is the responsibility of the business manager to see that the auditorium where the play is given is kept well ventilated at a comfortable temperature, and free from disturbing noises during rehearsals as well as at the public performance. In securing proper ventilation he will be careful to open windows upon one side of the auditorium only so as to avoid cross draughts.

All matters requiring attention in front of the curtain and not specifically given into the keeping of others are the responsibility of the business manager. So, if the stage electrician requests it, the business manager will hold himself responsible for the proper regulation of the auditorium lights. And so, too, he will secure the needed ushers *before* the day when they are actually needed and give them proper instructions as to their duties.

SUMMARY

The business manager, then, has several exacting responsibilities. First, he must secure a place or places for the play to be given and make sure of the exact day and hour in each case. He must also make a clear-cut financial agreement with every organization sponsoring a performance of the play. Second, if the play is to be given on a strange stage, he must inspect the stage and its equipment and report the same to the director, cast, and crew. He must also make sure of all routes of travel and the means and costs of transportation. Third, he must make advance arrangements for programs and for ushers for every performance. Fourth, he must see that the auditorium is kept well ventilated, at a comfortable temperature, and free from disturbing noises both during rehearsals and performances. And, lastly, he must be responsible for, and keep a full and accurate record of, all sums received and spent. He must make a complete report of the same to the director the day after each production.

CHECK LIST FOR BUSINESS MANAGER

1. Have you kept the Players' funds entirely separate from all others?
2. Have you made out a budget and is it balanced?
3. Have dates been secured for productions? (These dates should be completed three weeks before the first production.)
4. Has the financial arrangement with each church or organization been clear cut and in writing?
5. Have you paid the royalty to the publisher?
6. Have you inspected the stage and equipment of each church and reported same to director, cast, and crew?
7. Have you arranged for transportation?
8. Have you arranged for:
   (a) Programs
   (b) Ushers
   (c) Hymn books
   (d) Janitor service (including ventilation)
   (e) An opportunity for rehearsal on the stage a day or two before the production.
9. Have you made full and accurate record of all sums received and spent, and rendered a report to the director a day after each production?
10. Have you turned over to the director the balance, after paying all bills?

Chapter VII

STAGE MANAGEMENT

THE stage manager ranks second in command to the director. He is, in fact, the director's executive officer having oversight over all matters taking place *back of the front curtain*. He is responsible for stage sets, draperies, curtains, the placement of major properties, the cleanliness and order of all things both on and off stage, the shifting of scenes, and the operation of all off-stage effects other than electrical. He is also charged with the duty of seeing that all the actors as well as the members of the back-stage crew are in their proper places at the proper time and that the whole production runs according to schedule. During an actual performance of the play, while the director takes his place as an observer out in the auditorium, the stage manager assumes the full authority and responsibility of the director himself. Needless to say, the stage manager should not be chosen from among the actors if this can be avoided. A complete fulfilment of all his duties will require his entire time and attention. However, should the size of the group be so small that the stage manager must be chosen from the cast itself, then, by all means, let him have but a minor rôle in the play.

PREPARING THE STAGE SET

The stage manager's duties begin with the preparation of the stage set. Let him first read the play, noting all the author's descriptions and stage directions. In this reading he will try to enter into the spirit of the play and arrive at an understanding of its mood and purpose so that his setting may lend itself to both, for it is not enough that a setting be merely mechanically correct and adequate. Now, bearing these things in mind, he will try to visualize the set as it must be constructed upon the stage to be used. When his ideas have taken tangible form he will consult with the director. Later he will take his revised plans to the costumer who will be charged with designing costumes which will harmonize with the setting, to the electrician who will be charged with its effective lighting, and to the business manager who must allow the funds for its construction.

The stage manager will design his stage set as simply and inexpensively as possible while yet achieving the essential effects and making adequate provision for the action of the play. A more detailed discussion of stage settings will be found in the chapter on stage equipment.

Having once settled upon the plan of construction, the stage manager's responsibility is to see that the completed set is ready for use *in rehearsals* as early as possible. Meanwhile he must provide such temporary makeshift as will enable director and actors to locate the position and visualize the general nature of objects on the stage so that they may proceed with the preliminary rehearsals for blocking out the action of the play.

PLACEMENT OF MAJOR PROPERTIES

The stage manager places all major properties upon the stage, that is to say, all set pieces such as rocks and trees, and all furniture such as chairs, tables, stands, etc. (All smaller properties such as books, vases, desk telephones, etc., are the responsibility of the property manager.) In order to place these major properties with accuracy and efficiency, let him proceed as follows:

With pencil in hand he will read the play through noting down every needed property and grouping the properties according to acts.

Next, in consultation with the director, he will make diagrams of the stage showing the exact location of all properties act by act. In planning this arrangement he will bear several things in mind: (1) The furnished stage must present to the audience a pleasing picture having unity, balance, harmony, and proportion. (2) Large pieces of furniture must not be placed too far downstage where they will obscure the audience's vision of action taking place upstage. (3) All furniture must be so placed as to allow for important bits of action to be played on important areas of the stage. (4) All furniture must be placed with due regard for the speed of the action. For example, if a character must cross from one chair to another it makes a distinct difference in the tempo of the play whether the chairs be near or far apart.

With this all done the stage manager is now ready to procure the properties. With his lists in hand he begins his search. Many properties can be borrowed. Some few have to be rented and others made. In both of the latter cases the business manager will of course have to be consulted. The all important thing at this stage is that an exact record be kept indicating the owner of each property rented or borrowed. Such a record is invaluable when the play is over. *And let it be an invariable rule that all borrowed or rented properties shall be returned not later than the day following the production.*

For all properties which cannot be secured immediately the stage manager must provide substitutes for use at the very first rehearsal. But let him procure the actual properties which will be used in the final production as soon as is humanly possible so that the actors may become accustomed to their use.

KEEPING ORDER BEHIND THE CURTAIN

The stage manager is responsible for the cleanliness and order of all things back of the front curtain. In this he must be a good housekeeper. There must be a definite place for everything. Every article whether small or large must be returned to its proper place after use and the whole kept free from dust and litter. The stage manager must be on hand well in advance of the scheduled opening of each rehearsal or performance and have the stage set up exactly as needed. His delay in this would waste the time not only of the director but of every member of the cast. And following each rehearsal or performance the stage manager must clear the stage and return all things to their proper places.

SHIFTING SCENES

If a play requires a change of setting during its course, the stage manager must rehearse his stage crew until the shift can be made quickly and noiselessly. Long waits between acts or scenes break the emotional continuity of the play, while nothing is more disturbing to the illusion which the audience builds about a drama than the sound of hammering or the rolling of trucks behind the curtain. These scene rehearsals should be called at times separate from those of the regular rehearsals of the cast. They should be continued until every person concerned knows his exact responsibilities in the moving of every piece of scenery and the whole crew works together with silent efficiency.

THE OPERATION OF OFF-STAGE EFFECTS

The stage manager is responsible for the operation of all off-stage sound and scenic effects other than those electrical. Whether he operates them himself or delegates this task to a subordinate, he will take care to rehearse such effects during regular rehearsals until they coordinate perfectly with the action on the stage and are produced in the proper mood and with the right intensity.

OFF-STAGE NOISES

Thunder may be produced in several ways, by rolling a heavy shot over a wooden floor, by rumbling a bass drum with the palm of the hand, or by shaking a thunder sheet. The thunder sheet is a large thin piece of sheet iron suspended in the air by one end from a piece of rope so that it will vibrate freely. It is operated by vibrating it from the lower edge with the hand. In order to be convincing the thunder sheet must be of considerable size.

Shot or small pebbles swished about inside a round wooden cheese box imitate the sound of rain.

The sound of waves can be had by rubbing sandpaper-covered blocks of wood together with a rhythmic surge.

Wind effects can be produced by a rotating wooden cylinder stripped longitudinally with thin strips of wood so as to present a corrugated surface. A piece of rough canvas is attached to one side of the supporting framework and allowed to fall over the rotating cylinder, the free end of the canvas being weighted. The more rapidly the cylinder is turned by its crank and the tighter the canvas is stretched over it, the louder the wind will shriek. A heavy piece of silk similarly hung over a revolving cylinder is even better than the canvas, though more costly and less durable.

Bird whistles and train whistles can be bought from dealers handling orchestra supplies. Duck calls and crow calls can be found at the sporting goods stores. The violin can often be pressed into service for many weird offstage cries. The flapping of birds' wings can be simulated by holding the ends of a towel folded lengthwise, one in either hand, and snapping it, tight and loose, in rapid succession.

The effect of hoof beats can be had by tapping coconut shells in the rhythm of a galloping horse.

Pistol shots may be made by the firing of blank cartridges or the sharp slap of two boards.

The sound of a motor may be secured by idling a car in the street just outside the stage door and leaving the door open. Most sound effects profit by distance, and this is especially true in the case of motors and motor horns.

Off-stage singing had best be done by carefully rehearsed singers, but where this is particularly difficult a phonograph may be substituted.

Off-stage noises are treacherous elements of dramatic effect. A crude imitation is worse than none. Unless they can be made convincing they had best be omitted. They all require much practice.

DRAWING THE CURTAIN

A curtain drawn too late or too soon or pulled too slowly or too rapidly can do much to mar the effectiveness of any closing scene. Nor is the effect of an opening curtain unimportant. The stage manager will always rehearse the drawing of the curtains several times before the play is ready for production. As a rough general rule a quick curtain is used for farce and other light comedy, a medium curtain for comedy of a serious vein, and a slow curtain for tragedy. The particular speed, however, will always be determined by the director. The stage manager's job is to see that the curtain operates at the exact moment when it is wanted, at the rate of speed ordered, noiselessly and *unfailingly*. This requires practise at rehearsals.

RESPONSIBILITIES AT PERFORMANCES

At all performances the stage manager will do well to insist that every actor be made up, in costume, and waiting quietly in his appointed place at least fifteen minutes before the time scheduled for the opening curtain. A last-minute rush of many persons causes confusion. The stage manager may then quietly check with each holder of back-stage responsibility to be sure that every last detail has been made ready.

MOVING THE PLAY TO A STRANGE STAGE

Should the group later give the play in a strange auditorium, the stage manager has a few simple but important duties to perform. First, he will make a personal visit to inspect the stage to be used so that he knows in advance all of its equipment as well as its limitations and is prepared to meet the new conditions. Second, he will notify the business manager of the time when he wishes the properties, stage sets, and other needed equipment transported and will ask that officer to provide a truck or dray. And, third, he will be present to see that all is properly loaded. He will personally supervise the unloading as well, and the arrangement upon the new stage. Such simple and common-sense precautions will save a world of grief.

CHECK LIST FOR STAGE MANAGER

1. Have you made stage plot (one inch to the foot) showing location of all entrances and exits, doors, windows, and furniture?
2. Have you checked this with the director *before first rehearsal?*
3. Have you secured and erected the stage set including the hanging of the necessary draperies *before first rehearsal?*
4. Have you secured and placed in their proper positions all major items of furniture including rugs if needed?
5. Have you cooperated with Electrician and Costumer in the above to make sure that lighting and color schemes are harmonious and effective?
6. Have you accepted responsibility for
   (a) Orderliness and cleanliness of stage and set and wings —everything back of front curtain?
   (b) Proper functioning of front curtain, rehearsing its opening and closing at the exact moments required and at the right tempo?
   (c) Checking sight lines of audience—so that no action on stage is hidden from view of audience?
   (d) Operating off-stage noises, telephones, etc.?
   (e) Having the stage ready for every rehearsal so that the cast is not delayed?
   (f) Cleaning up stage, storing away draperies and furniture promptly after the last performance?

Chapter VIII

LIGHTING

THE lighting of a play for a church differs from the lighting of a play in a theatre in this important respect: the church auditorium, or parish hall, is usually much smaller than the theatre and the audience is proportionately closer to the stage. This means that less intense lights will be used for the church play. Where the theatre seating 1000 uses bulbs of 1000 to 1500 watts or more in its flood lights and spots, the church or parish hall seating 500 will use bulbs of 250 to 500 watts with similar reductions in the size of other lighting units. Otherwise the problems of lighting, its mysteries, and its beauties are the same in church and theatre.

THE PURPOSES OF STAGE LIGHTING

The purposes of stage lighting are eight:

First, lighting should give a proper degree of visibility to the setting and to the actors, especially to the actors' features. This must never be lost sight of in striving after other effects. Let the lighting be neither so dim as to strain the eye nor so glaring as to be painful. The happy medium is the goal.

Second, lighting should make both scene and actors stand out in three-dimensional form—height, breadth and depth. It should preserve the plastic elements of the picture—never flatten them.

Third, lighting should *appear* to come from natural sources such as the windows of an interior set if the scene be daylight, or visible lighting fixtures if it be night. If the scene be moonlight by all means let what shadows there be fall downward. Blue footlights should never be permitted to cast upward pointing shadows on the back drop.

Fourth, lighting should set the time of day or indicate other natural phenomena such as the approach of storms or the breaking of the moon through cloud banks.

Fifth, lighting should produce pleasing compositions of light and shade. The stage should seldom be lighted with equal intensity in all parts. Yet while shadows rightly placed may have a high pictorial or emotional value and serve to give plasticity to the scene, the electrician should beware of shadows which are unnatural or merely distracting. The unintended shadow is one of the stage electrician's most persistent enemies.

Sixth, lighting should reenforce the psychological elements of the play, should help to establish atmosphere and mood.

Seventh, lighting should pick out and emphasize the important acting areas of the stage.

And, eighth, lighting should bring out the desired colors of all painted scenery, in draperies, and costumes. Study of the effect which the light primaries, red, green, and violet, have upon various color pigments will help the electrician to achieve the color effects he desires, but nothing will take the place of actual experimentation with the lighting when the scene is set and the actors in costume.

SOURCES OF GENERAL ILLUMINATION

General illumination for the stage is drawn from three sources: border lights, strip lights, and footlights.

Border lights are made up of a row of electric bulbs screwed into receptacles placed in a reflecting trough which is hung overhead. The first or "concert" border is hung immediately above and behind the rectangular opening through which the audience views the stage—the proscenium arch. Other borders are hung parallel to this at seven foot intervals, the number depending upon the depth of the stage. All borders save the "concert" border are concealed behind "fly" curtains which hang down from above the playing area and extend just low enough to shield the borders and to prevent the gaze of the audience from wandering up into the space above the stage. Border lights serve a useful purpose in providing evenly distributed overhead illumination and do much to prevent unwanted shadows upon the walls. However, there is a tendency on many stages to discard the border lights in favor of a battery of small box floods and baby spots suspended from an iron pipe batten hung over the front of the stage in the position of the "concert" border. This is a satisfactory arrangement, especially if a ceiling piece is to be dropped down over the stage in place of the fly curtains in interior scenes.

Strip lights are similar troughs of lights held in an upright position on supporting standards. In use they stand in the off-stage space on either side of the playing area—the space technically known as "the wings." From there they cast a horizontal illumination inward upon the scene and serve to lighten the actors' faces and counterbalance the downward thrust of light from the borders.

Footlights are made up in exactly the same way as are borders and strips but are laid flat upon the floor at the front of the stage in a depression which conceals them from the audience. From this position their light is directed inward upon the stage and upward. Footlights, when used as a major source of illumination, destroy all natural shadows upon the faces of the actors and are not to be recommended. Their useful purpose is twofold: first, to help tie other lighting effects together by reducing too great contrasts, and, second, to soften the shadows upon the faces of actors playing far downstage. For this last purpose they should be used in connection with one or more large spotlights dimmed to low intensity and placed in a rear balcony or concealed in the upper part of the auditorium. The footlights alone, unbalanced by overhead illumination, always distort the features.

All borders, strips, and foots should be wired for at least a three-color combination of red, blue, and light amber bulbs in such fashion that each color is controlled by a separate electric circuit which is connected to its own dimmer in the switch board and clearly marked. In this way any one or two colors can be dimmed out independently of the remainder. A four-color combination is even better, in which case the bulbs should be of red, green, blue, and light amber.

Bulbs should be so spaced in border, strip, and footlights that those of the same color are not separated by more than twenty inches where a four-color combination is used, or fifteen inches where a three-color combination is used. When bulbs are widely separated there is a tendency toward spottiness of color on objects near the lights.

Although the cheaper type of light troughs in which

the colored bulbs are merely screwed into adjoining sockets will serve with a very fair degree of satisfaction, the best type is that in which each bulb is fitted into a separate reflecting compartment having a glass color screen and all are banked closely together.

SOURCES OF SPECIFIC ILLUMINATION

While good general illumination is necessary upon every stage, it is through the controlled lights and shades of specific illumination that the electrician finds his most expressive medium. Specific illumination is achieved by the use of spots and floods of varying sizes.

The *spot light* has a lens and a focusing device by which a concentrated beam of light can be trained on some specific spot. The large spots are supported on standards and are used to throw a light upon the stage from some distance. They should be equipped with color screens and, if possible, should have their own rhe· ostats, or dimmers, attached to the supporting standard. They should also have a switch which will allow the operator to turn the light off or on at will.

The *baby spots* are used upon the stage itself to secure small, concentrated areas of light from various angles and to produce contrasting shadows. The baby spot may be set upon a standard or hung from a pipe batten overhead. It is one of the most generally useful pieces of lighting equipment the electrician has. It also should be furnished with color screens.

The *flood light* gives an intense and diffused light over a limited area. The large flood is set upon a standard and is used to cast a flood of light from out of the wings. It is usually the source of the sunshine which pours in through the stage window. It should be fitted

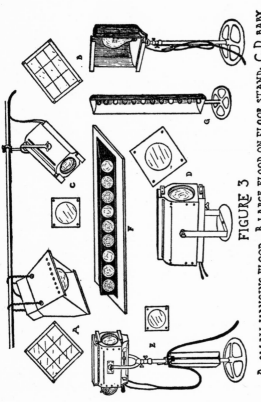

FIGURE 3

A, SMALL HANGING FLOOD, B, LARGE FLOOD ON FLOOR STAND, C, D, BABY SPOTS, E, LARGE SPOT ON FLOOR STAND, F, FOOT LIGHTS, CONCEALING TYPE WHICH DROPS FLUSH WITH STAGE FLOOR, BOXED, GLASS COLOR SCREENS, G, SIMPLE TROUGH STRIP LIGHT; COLOR SCREENS SHOWN WITH ALL LAMPS.

with color screens and its own switch and dimmer. The small box floods, like the baby spots, may be hung overhead from pipe battens. They should be equipped with color screens.

A technical description of the many types of floods and spots upon the market is not possible here. Let the electrician and business manager together consult the most recent volumes on amateur stage lighting. Let them also study the catalogues of reliable firms in the light of their own specific needs and the funds available. Where possible, let them secure the equipment upon approval, and try it out in actual operation before final purchase.

A MINIMUM LIGHTING EQUIPMENT

A minimum lighting equipment will consist of a row of first border lights, two portable strip lights for use from either side and behind the proscenium, a large spot light for use from the balcony, and one large flood light for use from the wings.

When increasing funds permit an expansion of this minimum equipment, one or two baby spots should be the first to be added. Next might come some of the small box floods. And, last of all, footlights might be installed.

THE SWITCH BOARD

The switch board should be located where the operator can at all times see the action upon the stage. It is best placed immediately to the rear and at one side or the other of the proscenium arch. If possible it should control auditorium lights as well as stage lights. It should also have banks of interlocking dimmers so that any one color of light upon the stage can be dimmed out separately or all can be dimmed out simultaneously. Moreover (point of importance!), its switches should all be of the *noiseless* variety. Toggle switches which are operated by pushing a little lever up or down with an accompanying sharp click, and rotary snap switches in which a knob is turned with the same clicking effect are an abomination upon the stage.

FLOOR PLUGS AND WIRING. CURRENT LOAD

Every stage should be equipped with at least three floor pockets into which portable lighting units can be plugged, one in the rear and one at each side of the playing space. These pockets should be capable of carrying a load equal to that demanded by the largest flood, usually 1500 to 2000 watts. All wiring should be done with rubber covered stage cable which meets the requirements of local electrical and fire ordinances. In determining the load which may safely be drawn through any one connection, let the electrician read the amperage and voltage which are noted upon every electric outlet. He will then multiply these two together. The product will be the maximum wattage which can safely be used from that connection. Now let him add the wattage of each electric bulb he plans to connect with that particular outlet and be sure that the total is a little below the product which he has already found as the maximum load for the connection in question.

WORKING OUT THE LIGHT PLOT

In working out the lighting plan (the light plot) for any play, the electrician will do well to begin with his sources of specific illumination. Let him first work out his areas of special emphasis and his main composition of lights and shadows. Then, when this has been done to his satisfaction, let him gradually bring up his general illumination to that point of intensity which best ties the whole composition together and gives the proper degree of visibility. He will do this by bringing on the lights of borders, strips, and foots very gradually, controlling them through the dimmer banks upon the switch board. He will test out his work with actors upon the stage, observing from every part of the auditorium their features and the general effect which he has produced.

LIGHT REHEARSALS

If the play requires any variation of the lighting during the course of the action, the electrician should call special light rehearsals. At these rehearsals the actors will go through their parts while he manipulates the lights to secure the proper effects at the proper times. When he has discovered the exact correlation between his work and the action upon the stage, he will carefully mark his copy of the script to indicate the various lighting effects as he is to produce them. He will do this by underlining certain speeches as light cues and making marginal notes as to the mechanics of handling the lights when this cue is heard. Thereafter he will carefully practise securing these effects at every rehearsal of the play.

COLOR AND EMOTION IN STAGE LIGHTING

Colored light has a pronounced emotional effect. The following hints may be of suggestive value, but in stage lighting nothing can take the place of actual experimentation.

Red is exciting and also tragic. Amber is warm and

cheerful. Yellow in small, concentrated areas reminds us of the light of the sun and brings a note of optimism. Likewise green when reflected from foliage or when used in small areas is the color of growing things and brings hope. But a general spread of yellow light causes actors to have a jaundiced appearance and suggests ill health. Likewise a general spread of green gives a ghastly, unearthly effect. Blue, when reflected from a daylight sky drop brings joy and hope, but as a general illumination it is cold and cheerless. Purple is the color of suffering. Greys and browns keep company with sadness.

The color of light may also suggest the time of day. A flood of yellow light entering a window suggests the full light of the sun. A cold blue-white suggests the light of early morning. Pink and red and burnished gold are the colors of sunset. Steel blue is used for moonlight.

Color is of value in centering attention upon a particular spot upon the stage. A small area of intense color cast in the midst of more or less neutral surroundings draws the eye as a magnet attracts steel.

Shadows too have color. In nature this color of the shadow tends toward the complement of the light which casts it. Thus, a red light will cast a greenish shadow. This should be observed in relation to scene painting. Scenic artist and electrician must always work in cooperation. Moreover, actual stage shadows which are cast by a brilliant light may have their density softened by other subdued light of a complementary color. A color wheel which will aid in determining complementary colors will be found in the following chapter on costuming.

Finally, the electrician must try out all of his color schemes in actual practise to learn their effect upon costumes, draperies, and scenery. This must never be left to the conclusions of abstract reasoning upon the basis of color theory. The electrician, the scene painter, and the costumer must try out their effects together.

CHECK LIST FOR ELECTRICIAN

1. Have you a tool kit equipped with: friction tape, electric plugs, fuses, extra wiring, screw driver, pliers, knife, small hammer, insulated staples, flash light, leather or rubber washers and clamps for spots and floods?
2. Have you extra bulbs for all necessary lighting units?
3. Have you made a lighting plot and submitted it to the director within the first week after you were appointed to this position on the crew?
4. Have you checked all electrical connections to make certain that there are no loose ones that might cause short circuits?
5. Have you experimented with the lights while actors are on the stage as well as between rehearsals, so as to determine proper angles, intensities, and color combinations?
6. Have you turned on the lights to be used before every rehearsal and turned them off immediately after it?
7. When the play is moved to a strange stage
    (a) Have you made a personal visit to the stage early enough to explore its lighting possibilities?
    (b) Have you taken along whatever equipment was necessary and brought it home again?
8. Have you observed the following admonitions:
    (a) Take nothing for granted. See and test all electrical items yourself.
    (b) Don't delegate work to another unless you first show him exactly what you want done, and know that he is dependable. And even then, remember that you have not delegated *responsibility*.
9. After the last production have you turned over to the director your electrician's tool kit complete with all equipment?

Chapter IX

COSTUMING

In his *Art of Play Production,* Professor John Dolman, Jr., tells us that costume had its origin in primitive ritual and that its first motive was symbolism, its second disguise; representation and impersonation developing later. This basic place of symbolism and of the element of suggestion in costuming is an important thing to remember, since the too great stressing of exact representation is apt to lead to much useless fretting and wasted effort. The whole matter is made clear in the following suggestive report from an advanced student.

COSTUMING A PLAY, NOT A PERIOD

The Deathless World with its scene laid several hundred years in the future was a very different play from any I had ever costumed. At first I tried to think in terms of what might be actually worn in the future judging by the development in the past. But I soon gave that up. In six hundred years there would be time either to go back to the elaborate and ponderous garments of Queen Elizabeth or to return to the simplicity of the Greeks. The men might even be wearing skirts and the women wearing trousers. I finally decided that this was one time when historicity did not count, that after all it was the play I was costuming, not a period.

According to the playwright the people of the time had lost great poetry and great emotions. From that I thought that painting and probably music would also have been lost.

And, if that were true, beautiful colors would not be used. All life would have sunk to an even plane with very few highlights of emotional interest. The best portrayal of this feeling in color is a black and white color scheme, and this is what I used. Margaret only, I put in color, since she had a more intense emotional life and expressed the spirit of revolt.

I chose the Greek style for Margaret's garment, making it an exact Doric chiton of a delicate lavender color. A conventional border of gold was the trimming which was stenciled around the entire edge.

For Guy I thought the Greek tunic too primitive, so I arbitrarily picked a soft white blouse from one period and full black trousers from another with a sash which was saved from being Spanish by not letting the ends hang and not making it all red.

The Wardens of the Holy Food I put in white, because they were "clean," so to speak.

The Doctor I put in black with white at the neck for pure conventionality.

The Servant of the Dead I put in a drab colored gown trimmed with black and made in a long, periodless fashion. She wore a black hooded cloak to suggest mourning.

My experience in this production taught me the need to costume a play from the play out instead of from a period in.

DETERMINING BASIC PATTERNS AND LINES

Yet all of this is not to belittle the proper place of historic accuracy in costuming. It would be most disconcerting to see a biblical drama played in the tunics and chitons of the Greeks or a play of the eighteenth century given in modern dress. For every play laid in an historic period it is the costumer's duty to give the audience an historically accurate impression—but an *impression* only, not a museum of burdensome detail.

The costumer will accomplish this purpose by careful study into the dress of the period involved. This study will reveal certain basic patterns for the various garments then worn and will reveal the characteristic silhouette of each. Thus, for the Hebrew of Bible days there will be found the long, loose coat, the wide girdle, the loose cloak, the sandals, the veil of the women and the turban of the men. If the costumer will fix these general guide points in mind, she may feel free to work a wide variety of costuming effects within their limits. She will bend her main efforts toward dramatic effectiveness rather than antiquarian detail. The possession of some good illustrated book upon historic costuming will be found invaluable in determining these basic patterns and silhouettes for the various periods. For the beginner one such book is *Costuming a Play* by Grimball and Wells, published by the Century Company.

COLOR COMBINATIONS

The planning of color schemes in the costuming will be carried out with regard to the entire stage picture quite as much as to individual costumes. The costumes of the actors must not clash with the colors used in the background nor with each other but must contribute to a pleasing and meaningful whole. Moreover, if the background is dark the costumes will need to be done in brighter hues so as to stand out in contrast. If the background is light the costumes will need to be darker.

Color should be applied so as to emphasize the importance of principal characters and subordinate minor ones. In general this will be done by reserving the more striking hues for the chief personages of the play, the more quiet ones for those of less importance. Further, this use of color to indicate relationships will usually result in the dressing of those characters who are in conflict in contrasting (but not clashing) hues.

Color will also be used in keeping with the personalities of the various characters to be costumed. A motherly old woman will hardly be dressed in flaming red nor a young girl in dull gray. Yet sometimes this basic consistency is purposely violated in order to secure special effects. Thus, in Lulu Vollmer's *Sun Up,* sympathy for the little girl is secured by dressing her in dull drab and having her long for a dress of color.

And, lastly, color will be used for its suggestive value to help establish mood. A play of stern, somber conflict and frustrated hopes will be costumed in dark tones and hues while a gay play will use bright colors.

For general guidance in working out color harmonies and contrasts the color wheel (page 121) adapted from Professor Dolman's *Art of Play Production* will be found useful.

Color contrast is obtained by using a color with its complementary, such as red with green. Color harmonies are obtained by combining colors which lie adjacent to each other or at least closely grouped upon the wheel. If colors which are not closely grouped and yet are separated by less than ninety degrees are combined, they are very apt to clash badly.

All color combinations must be tried out under the actual stage lighting to be used. Wasteful experiments may be avoided by draping the uncut fabrics under the lighting to be used upon the completed costumes. Let the costumer and the electrician confer together over the effects desired and those actually produced. Often the electrician can remedy an undesirable effect at this stage by a slight alteration of his lighting.

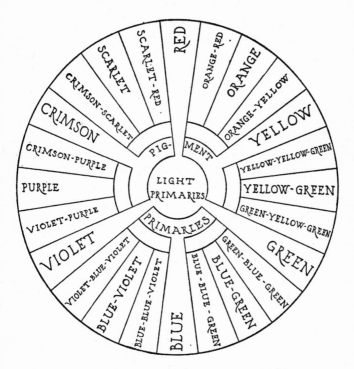

FIGURE 4 - COLOR WHEEL

CHOICE OF FABRICS

Materials must be considered as to weave, weight, and surface texture. It is seldom necessary to use highly expensive fabrics for stage costumes. Usually a cheaper fabric can be so treated with dye and lighting as to be an effective substitute. However, in making such substitutions the draped lines in which the substitute fabric falls must be considered quite as much as the appearance of the surface.

In choosing the fabrics for particular costumes the costumer will, of course, as in the case of color, be guided by the comparative importance of the character. She will also consider the times in which the character is supposed to live and his social and economic status. Price lists and samples of fabrics from firms dealing in costuming material for the stage will prove both money-saving and suggestive. Let the costumer also learn to delight herself in the bargain basements of department stores and learn the mysteries of the dye pot.

CARING FOR THE COSTUMES

A mussed or soiled costume should never be permitted upon the stage. At every dress rehearsal and performance the costumer will see that each actor's costume is in proper readiness and that it is carefully marked with an identifying tag and hung in the costume wardrobe afterward. Needless to say, when a play is over, costumes should be cleaned and pressed before being packed away for future use.

The costumer will also be responsible for the prompt return in good order of all borrowed or rented costumes on the day following the performance.

THE COSTUME WARDROBE

Any church drama group will do wisely if it establishes a costume wardrobe where costumes can be safely protected from injury and kept against future need. Costumes from one play may be altered and dyed for another at great saving in expense. The costumer should solicit contributions of discarded draperies, interesting old suits and hats and shoes and dresses, and pack them away in the wardrobe. In time this will become a valuable asset if kept neatly and well.

HELPING THE ACTOR

But the costumer's job does not end with the mere planning, preparation and care of the costumes. She should be helpful to the players themselves in their use of the garments she has prepared. Let her then have all costumes ready as early as possible so that the actors may have time to accustom themselves to their strange clothing and become at ease in it. One dress rehearsal is not enough for this, especially if the clothing is not modern. Let her also give attention to each individual actor to see that his costume fits properly, that he is comfortable in it, and, in so far as possible, that he is pleased with it. And, lastly, let the costumer always be prepared with needle and thread and scissors and pins (especially an ample supply of safety pins!) to meet all last-minute emergencies.

Chapter X

MAKE-UP

THERE is but one final way in which to learn the art of make-up for plays to be presented in churches and that is by actual experimentation in applying the materials of make-up to human faces. The actor may as well expect to master the piano by the mere reading of instruction books without the hours of practise required as to learn make-up by reading books only. This chapter, then, is to be used solely as a laboratory manual, a suggestive guide sheet, while the user learns by doing.

THE WHY OF MAKE-UP

The purpose of make-up is simply this: to make the player's features seem *natural* to the audience. Two factors work against this natural effect—the un-natural lighting and the distance of the audience from the player. If the first were the only one the question would naturally arise: Why not work to make the lighting natural instead of putting make-up on the actor's face? The answer is that if the lighting were reduced to the natural lighting of the scene in real life the features of the actor would hardly be visible at the distance at which a large part of the audience must sit. To make the features of the player visible at a distance, therefore, requires more intense lighting, and more intense lighting throws the features and the colors out of proportion. Hence the need of make-up.

WARNING

Beware of too much make-up! It is much better to have too little. But most amateurs err on the side of too much. This is especially true in religious drama where the distance of the players from the audience is much shorter and the lighting much less subtle than in the average theatre or even in a school auditorium.

Beware, too, of the guidance of professional actors in make-up. They probably know far more about make-up for the theatre than the amateur in religious drama will ever know. But the professional actor has been trained for the lighting and the distances in the theatre. These are greater in the theatre than in the church or parish house and the professional actor seems usually to forget this and to over-do the make-up. It should be kept subdued, so subdued that no one in the audience twenty-five feet or more away will ever be conscious that any make-up is in use.

STRAIGHT MAKE-UP

In general, there are two kinds of make-up: Straight and Character. Straight make-up is that used when the player assumes a rôle requiring physical features or age not unlike his own. Character make-up is that used when the player must assume a part whose physical features or age are considerably different from his own.

To apply a straight make-up, the first step is the application of a liberal coating of theatrical cold cream to face and neck and ears. This must be well worked into the pores of the skin and the surplus then wiped off with cleansing tissue. The surface of the skin should be left quite dry, especially about the eyes and nostrils. The purpose of this cold cream is to provide a base for the grease paint over which it may be smoothly spread and also to prevent the grease paint from being absorbed into the pores of the skin itself.

The actor will then apply his foundation color. For a man this will be juvenile if a blond, or juvenile deeper shade if a brunette. For a woman this will be pink if a blonde, or juvenile if a brunette. The actor will take this stick of foundation color and make two marks across the forehead, two down either cheek and one down the nose, a mark across the chin, and one down either side of the throat. The color should then be spread with the finger tips and blended until the entire face, the ears, and the neck are covered by a smooth, even film of color. Especial care should be taken to work this color well up into the roots of the hair so that no white line shows at the base of the hair.

Next the actor will heighten the color of the cheeks and lips by the application of moist rouge. Both blonde and brunette men will use a medium shade. Blonde women will use a light shade, brunettes the medium. This rouge is applied with the finger tip.

In youth the color spot is high on the cheek bones. As age advances this color spot sinks lower upon the cheek and becomes roughly triangular. Let the actor apply the rouge in its full intensity to the center of the color spot and then spread it out, working out from and around that center. The edges of the color spot must be so blended into the foundation color that no line of demarcation is left.

The lips must be made up with care so as not to make them appear too wide or full. Nor should the color of

the lips be too intense. The rouge is applied to the center of the lips first and worked outward. The inner edges
of the lips must be made up as well as the visible portions so as to avoid color contrasts when the lips are
parted in smiling or talking. It is seldom advisable to
make up the lips all the way to the corners since such
treatment tends to widen the mouth. Women may accentuate the cupid's bow of the upper lip slightly. Men
must be careful not to rouge either lips or cheeks too
highly.

Now the eyes must be accentuated. If the stage is at
all brilliantly lighted the eyes will need to be shadowed.
Blondes will use a medium blue eye shadow or grease
paint for this, brunettes a dark brown. Women with
hazel eyes may use a blue-green blended according to
the light under which they are to work. The actor will
apply a very light film of the color with the finger tip to
the upper lid only, blending it upward to where the lid
folds under the fulness above the eye, and outward
toward the outer edge of the lids until it fades into the
foundation color. Now, with the tip of a smooth wooden
toothpick which has been drawn through dark brown
lining color, the actor will draw fine lines just outside
the points where the eyelashes meet the eyelids. On the
upper lid the line will begin well beyond the middle
of the eye toward the nose and be extended a fraction
of an inch beyond the outer corner and sloping gently
downward. On the lower lid the line will begin at the
middle of the eye and be extended straight out a fraction of an inch beyond the point where the lower lid
curves upward. A third line is then drawn to connect the
two at the farthest point on the upper line. Avoid giving
a too obviously triangular effect. Next a small dot of
the moist rouge is placed with a toothpick just outside

the inner corner of the eye. This treatment makes the eyes appear both larger and brighter. Women may further make up their eyelashes with mascara or cosmetic, but this may be omitted in a small auditorium where the actors are close to the audience.

When all this has been done *in the order given*,[1] and not before, then the actor is ready to apply powder. The men will use juvenile flesh powder, as will also the brunette women. Blonde women will use natural flesh powder. The powder should be used freely upon a powder puff and *patted*, not rubbed, into the make-up. Let the actor continue to pat the powder into the make-up until it has absorbed as much as it will hold. Then the surplus should be lightly brushed off. A baby's hair brush is ideal for this purpose but the powder puff itself may be used.

The straight make-up is completed by touching up the color spots on the cheeks with dry rouge and by touching the lips with the tongue to remove the powder from them. The men will use raspberry dry rouge; blonde women will use light dry rouge; brunette, #18 theatrical dry rouge.

The colors given above for grease paint, liners, rouge, and powder for the various types will be found generally satisfactory. However, people who are excessively light or dark may wish to experiment under the stage lights until they find shades more exactly suited to their individual types. The essential thing is that those colors be used which fit the type rather than to have in the kit

---

[1] When, however, grease paint has been used for shadows on the eyelids it should be instantly powdered lightly so that it will not smudge the surface above the eyelid when the eye opens and the lid folds in. The enlarging lines about the eyes are usually best not powdered at all, so that they may be distinct and carry.

one fixed set of colors to be used upon everyone regardless of natural complexion.

CHARACTER MAKE-UP

The order of procedure in character make-up is exactly the same as in straight although differing colors are used and certain special effects are added.

In making up for age let the actor remember that as the body ages the skin loses its freshness and takes on a yellow tone; the eyes become dull and sunken; the color spot on the cheeks sinks lower and tends toward a triangular shape while the color is both paler and duller than in youth; the cheeks themselves become sunken; the lips grow thin and pale and withered; the mouth often drops, and the face becomes lined with wrinkles. The following combinations of make-up material are suggested for securing effects of middle years and age:

MIDDLE-AGED MAN

Orange grease paint
Medium moist rouge
Dark brown liner for sunken effects
Yellow or white liner for high lights
Dark brown or maroon for eye shadow
Neutral face powder
Natural dry rouge

MIDDLE-AGED WOMAN

Cream grease paint
Medium moist rouge
Dark brown liner for sunken effects
Yellow or white liner for high lights
Blue-gray liner for eye shadow
Neutral face powder
Natural dry rouge

OLD MAN

Orange grease paint
Medium moist rouge

OLD WOMAN

Yellow grease paint
Medium moist rouge

Dark brown liner for sunken effects	Dark brown liner for sunken effects
Yellow or white liner for high lights	Yellow or white liner for high lights
Dark brown or maroon liner for eye shadow	Dark brown or maroon liner for eye shadow
Light cream powder	Neutral face powder
Use no dry rouge	Theatrical dry light rouge

Eyes are sunken by blending in the dark brown lining color between the upper lids and the eyebrows and also below the eyes, and upon the lids. The shading below the eyes should be circular, following the line of the eye-socket itself, which can be felt easily by the finger. Coloring the edges of the lids next the lashes with white will dull the eyes. A red line here will give a watery and weak appearance.

Cheeks are sunken by blending a touch of dark brown lining color into the cheek and then highlighting the cheek bone.

Lips may be thinned by covering them with the foundation color and then carefully wiping it away from the inner edges until the desired width shows. As a general rule no lip color is needed for old age, although a bit of blue mixed with lip rouge may sometimes be used to good advantage. Lips are shriveled by drawing fine vertical lines across them with a smooth wooden toothpick rubbed through the dark brown lining color. These vertical lines may be extended slightly beyond the red of the lip and highlighted by white lines drawn beside them and carefully blended by the finger. This will increase the shriveled effect.

Wrinkles should follow the natural lines of the face. These can be determined easily by wrinkling the forehead, squinting the eyes and grimacing with the mouth.

Especial care should be taken that the wrinkles about the eye do not radiate out from a common point at the outer corner of the eye as many amateur actors draw them. They should not be less than a quarter of an inch apart at the corner of the eye. All wrinkles should be laid on in very fine lines with the point of a smooth wooden toothpick, slightly coated with the lining color. This line should then be blended with the foundation color by rubbing lightly over it with the tip of the little finger. The ends of all wrinkle lines should be blurred into indistinctness by the tip of the finger. Every wrinkle line should be highlighted to give it the appearance of depth, by drawing a line of lighted color beside it—above it for the nostril lines, below it for crows-feet and frown lines. The highlight should be three or four shades lighter than the foundation color. In making up for age this will usually call for white or yellow. The highlights are then also blended into the foundation color by rubbing lightly over them with the tip of the little finger until no sharp lines of demarcation show.

To gray the eyebrows white grease paint or liner is rubbed into them. If a shaggy effect is wanted, the eyebrow is then rubbed the wrong way with the finger tip.

When all of the grease paint effects are laid on, the make-up is then set by patting it full of powder just as was done for the straight make-up. The shades of powder to use with the middle-aged man, middle-aged woman, old man and old woman are given in the combinations suggested above. The powder used with any make-up should approximate the color of the grease paint used as the foundation. The powder must be so light in shade and applied so gently and sparingly as not to obscure the wrinkles and other effects so laboriously secured.

Beards and mustaches are made of crêpe hair which may be purchased in foot lengths in any shade desired. This hair is first unbraided from the strings. Next, with a coarse comb it is combed out from the end. The hair will mat into the teeth of the comb and be left hanging from one side in short lengths. When the comb is full the hair is slid off the teeth and the matted ends are clipped off with the shears. When sufficient hair for the beard has been prepared in this way, and fluffed out ready for applying, the actor lays a coating of spirit gum over a small portion of the face where the beard naturally grows. He then quickly applies the fluffed-out hair to his face by sticking the clipped ends to the spirit gum and pressing them firmly into place. The spirit gum dries very quickly and should be applied only to a small area at a time. It will not stick well on grease paint.

In applying the hair to the face it is best to begin at the point of the chin and then work upward. The beard should not be laid on too close to the ears. The actor must observe the natural hair line as it approaches the ears and also as it approaches the lower lip and follow it. Care should be taken to bring the hair well down on the under side of chin and jaws.

The mustache is best laid on in two sections a quarter inch apart from the center of the upper lip outward to either side. Care should be taken to follow the natural droop of the upper lip.

When the beard is completed, it is then carefully trimmed into the desired shape, using the shears just as if it were a natural beard.

Other special effects may be secured in various ways.

By modeling nose putty over the features before any cold cream or foundation color has been applied, the size and shape of both nose and chin may be completely altered. The shape of the nose may also be modified by the application of highlights and shadows. Teeth may be blacked out by coating them with black wax. The face may be made cheerful or sad by extending the corners of the mouth slightly up or down. Eyes may be slanted by drawing the lines upward at the outer corners and by blocking out the outer portion of the natural eye-brow with foundation color and painting a slanting brow with the suitable lining color.

Hair is best grayed by the use of corn starch applied with a powder puff. When wigs are used great care should be taken to see that they fit properly and that they are kept clean and well dressed.

When the face is heavily made up for character effects, other exposed portions of the body are made up to match. A sunburned face and lily-white hands are not convincing. Nor are a wrinkled face and plump, smooth hands.

A SPECIAL WORD OF CAUTION

The actor should try out all make-up under the actual stage lighting and have others criticize the effect from various parts of the auditorium. And let him remember that too much make-up is worse than none at all.

AN IDEAL MAKE-UP KIT

It is ideal when each actor can have his own individual make-up kit which is stocked with just the range of colors best suited to his own type, but this can seldom be done. An adequate church make-up kit will have a supply of all the various colors of paint and rouge and powder mentioned in the above suggestions concerning differing types of make-up. It will also contain theatrical cold cream, cleansing tissue for removing make-up, towels to place around the neck while making up, a supply of smooth wooden toothpicks, powder puffs, a mirror, a comb for combing out crêpe hair, a pair of shears, lengths of crêpe hair in several shades, a bottle of spirit gum, nose putty, corn starch, and Ivory soap. Such a kit can be stocked completely for ten dollars.

A MINIMUM ASSORTMENT OF MAKE-UP MATERIALS

If necessity dictates, the following assortment of paints, rouge, and powder can be substituted with a fair degree of satisfaction for the complete range mentioned above:

Grease paints: pink, juvenile, sallow old age.

Liners: blue, brown, gray, white.

Rouge: light moist and light and medium dry.

Powder: juvenile flesh and sallow old age.

The nose putty may also be omitted. The other supplies are necessities. Such a reduced kit could be stocked for five or six dollars.

A WORD TO THE MAKE-UP MANAGER

When the actors themselves are untrained in the art of make-up so that the make-up manager is responsible for making up the entire cast, he should allow at least twenty minutes per person for the task. It will be well, if the cast is at all large, for him to train several assistants, but he himself must exercise final judgment over their work and so organize their efforts as to avoid confusion. Let the make-up manager try out all make-ups in rehearsal. Let him further check the contents of the make-up kit before the night of the performance, so that every item needed will surely be on hand ready to use. *And let him clean the make-up box and its contents after every use.*

For a more comprehensive treatment of this difficult subject the reader is referred to John F. Baird's *Make-Up*.[2]

[2] Published by Samuel French, $1.50.

Chapter XI

PROPERTIES

THERE is a widely prevalent opinion among amateurs that properties are relatively unimportant and can be secured at the last moment, after but little thought, and then left to take care of themselves. The exact opposite is true. Properties are a highly important aid to good acting. They require considerable thought in their selection. They should be on hand at an early rehearsal. They should be kept in order and available during the period of their use. And *immediately* the play is over they should be returned to their owner if borrowed, or safely stored away if made or purchased.

THE PURPOSE OF PROPERTIES

Properties are used in at least four distinct ways:

First, they are an aid to the actor in performing convincing pantomime. Mis' Abel's flat-iron in Zona Gale's comedy, *The Neighbors*, is of immense value. To see Mis' Abel's vigorous, decided strokes with that iron is to learn worlds about the character of Mis' Abel shortly after the curtain rises. Later to see the listless, absent-minded strokes of Inez as she uses the same iron, and to see her finally slam it down in impatience with Peter's tongue-tied helplessness, that is to learn the truth about Inez' love for Peter.

Second, properties may symbolize the spirit of a play, or of a character, or of a particular bit of action. In Margaret Larkin's play, *El Cristo*, the rough wooden benches and table and the rude wooden crosses symbolize the spiritual crucifixion of José which forms the theme of the play.

Third, properties may convey information and provide background. When, into an atmosphere of foreboding in Karel Capek's *R. U. R.*, there is introduced Helena's discovery of the pistol in her husband's coat pocket, the implications fairly leap at the audience. The Robots are in revolt. There is immediate danger of an attack. Helena had been kept in ignorance to prevent loading useless worries upon her.

Fourth, properties are used to add characteristic elements of beauty or interest to the stage picture. Such is the purpose of the brazier and of the pottery jars in Mary P. Hamlin's play, *He Came Seeing*.

PREPARING PROPERTY LISTS

The property manager upon being assigned his job will first study the play so as to learn its mood and setting and the circumstances and tastes of the various characters. This is necessary in order that the properties secured may be in harmony with the play and help make its meaning clear. As he reads he will carefully note down every object which the actors use, exclusive of the heavier pieces of furniture such as tables and chairs which are the responsibility of the stage manager. All properties which are picked up, handled, or carried about should be noted down. He will do well to make two such lists. The first one should be arranged in a continuous column on the page with space left after every item for notes. In this space the property manager will carefully write down the source from which

each property is secured *at the time when he secures it.*
Later, as he returns each property to its rightful owner,
he will write down also the date of its return. This list,
with every item properly accounted for, should be given
to the director not later than the second day following
the final performance of the play. The second list should
tell exactly where each property belongs upon the stage,
and when it is to be used in the course of the play. If
the play is full length, this listing should be done by
acts.

The first list will guide in securing the needed properties and in their prompt return. The second will guide
in placing the properties during rehearsals and performances and will prevent slips. Below are samples of
such lists:

LIST OF PROPERTIES FOR *HE CAME SEEING*

(A check-list for their proper securing and return)

Brass bowl—Borrowed from Mrs. Bremmicker (Returned
Feb. 12)
Brazier—From properties on hand (In Store Room)
Stand for brazier—Borrowed from Mr. Weage (Returned
Feb. 12)
Charcoal—From properties on hand (In Store Room)
Box of rosin—From properties on hand (In Store Room)
Two pieces of crude pottery—Purchased from Coover Stu-
dios, 19 N. Wabash Ave. (In Store Room)
Gilded vase—From properties on hand (In Store Room)
Pottery vase—Borrowed from Mrs. Weage (Returned
Feb. 12)
Shepherd's staff—Rented from Schmidt Costume Co., 920
N. Clark St. (Rented Feb. 5 Returned Feb. 10)
(Rented Feb. 12 Returned Feb. 14)
Barley cakes—(pasteboard) (In Store Room)

LIST OF PROPERTIES FOR *THE TINKER*

(A guide-list for placing properties on stage)

ACT I:

In readiness at left entrance:

A newspaper,

A story magazine,

A package of letters and postal cards—among them one in a long envelope,

A postman's whistle,

A telephone bell with electric battery,

Jane and Marjorie's baggage,

Christmas boxes; tissue paper and holiday ribbons; a gavel; a lace collar; phonograph record; cut glass bowl; box such as might contain a pair of socks and a necktie; two small books, in one of which is folded a small card.

In readiness at right entrance:

Tinker's tool kit containing small screw driver, pliers, knife, etc.,

An apron, a polishing cloth and a large spoon for Jack,

A dish towel for Ethel.

On the stage:

Math book and clutter of papers on table L.R.,

Telephone on stand L.L.,

Clock on mantel with bogus works concealed behind it,

Water jug and glass on mantel.

Tinker must be sure to have small silver in pocket.

(Properties for Acts II and III listed in similar fashion.)

DUTIES OF THE PROPERTY MANAGER

The property manager is responsible for having all properties on hand for use in rehearsals as early as possible. If the actual properties themselves cannot be secured by the time of the first rehearsal, he must provide suitable substitutes which will aid the actor in determining his stage business with the property in question. The property manager is also responsible for seeing that every property is properly placed upon the stage before every rehearsal and performance, and stored away in proper order afterwards. *And he is responsible for the safe return of all properties not later than the day following the final performance.*

CHECK LIST FOR PROPERTY MANAGER

1. Have you made out a complete list of all properties needed in this play?
2. Have you secured them promptly so that they were on hand and ready for use by the second rehearsal?
3. Have you noted on your list:
   (a) Where each item was obtained and when and from whom?
   (b) When each item is to be returned and to whom?
   (c) Where each item is to be placed upon the stage during rehearsals and public performances?
   (d) Where each item is to be stored between rehearsals?
4. Have you given a copy of this list to the director?
5. Have you seen to it that all items were in their proper places upon the stage before each rehearsal and public performance?
6. Have you notified each player where to find his property items before making his entrance?
7. Have you returned all the properties, with the thanks of the players, promptly after the final performance?

Chapter XII

PUBLICITY

A GOOD play deserves a large audience. Moreover, players cannot be expected to do their best before a poorly filled auditorium. There is a give and take between actors and audience which is absolutely essential to the success of any play. Nor can a play succeed financially without a sizable audience. This last holds even more true of a production when no admission price is charged. The nickels and dimes are apt to predominate in any free will offering. It takes a goodly number of these to pay the average five dollar royalty fee plus the expense for costumes, play books and what-not. And the responsibility for securing the audience rests largely upon the shoulders of the publicity manager. He should, there-fore, use every dignified avenue which his ingenuity can suggest for giving the play effective publicity. Among these avenues will be at least the following:

THE NEWS STORY

Most editors of newspapers are glad to use a well-written news story. However, the publicity manager must not expect to submit an extravagantly worded "blurb" or a rambling account and get it printed. The editor's time is crowded. He wants only that material which has news value for his readers, and he wishes it written with brevity, conciseness, and vigor. Moreover, he must have it in his hands on time. In this latter regard it is well to note that most large city newspapers have a religious editor whose job it is to run a special page of church news every Saturday. Where this is the case the publicity manager will do well to send his news story directly to the religious editor. The story should reach this editor's desk by Wednesday since such pages are usually set up well in advance of the day of their actual publication.

The very first paragraph of the news story should answer these five questions: What is the play? Who is giving it? Where? When? Why? Succeeding paragraphs should add supplementary items of interest in the order of their importance, taking into account the fact that, if the story be too long to fit the editor's available space, he will cut it paragraph by paragraph, beginning at the end.

In general the publicity manager will seek to tell those things about the play and its production which have interest value for the general reader. In the case of a royalty play he will give credit to both author and publisher. He will make his sentences short, simple, and vigorous. He will use a typewriter, write on one side of the page only, begin his story a third of the way down the page, leave wide margins, double space the lines, and omit the title, writing in its place simply NEWS ITEM in caps. At the left upper corner of the first page he will place his own name, address and phone number. At the right upper corner he will note the number of words in the news story. No other comment is necessary.

THE CHURCH BULLETIN

The bulletins mailed or given into the hands of the congregation by the ushers are a valuable means of publicity. Announcements intended for the church bulletin should be short and simple, including only those items of information which are essential. They should be in the pastor's hands by the middle of the week preceding unless other instructions are noted in the bulletins themselves. In churches which do not print bulletins a short notice should be prepared for oral announcement by the pastor. It is well to use the church bulletin at least two successive Sundays in advance of the play.

THE POSTER

Posters can be a very valuable means of publicity if thought and care go into their making.

The first requirement of a good poster is that it catch the eye and be easily readable. The perfect poster will be clearly legible from a distance of at least twenty feet. Let the designer remember that the poster is used in public places where it must catch and hold the attention of busy passers-by. Plain block letters laid on in India ink with a printing pen are best.

Second, a good poster will include all essential information. It will answer the Who? What? Where?— and When? Sometimes it will also answer the Why? It will include acknowledgment to author and publisher in the case of all royalty plays, although the more important spaces of the poster need not be sacrificed to this purpose. *But the good poster will never be cluttered.* The passer-by should be able to take in its whole import as he walks along. Let the designer choose only those items of greatest interest value, arrange them as attractively as possible, and do all briefly and to the point.

Pictures are valuable if they really illustrate, and color

is always an aid. Mere garishness is to be avoided, as are the clashes of inharmonious coloring. But the use of the more vivid hues and the employment of color contrasts aid in compelling attention.

The size of the poster will be regulated by the place in which it is to be displayed. An outside bulletin board will often permit a poster as large as thirty-six by fifty-four inches, but merchants seldom want their store windows blocked by rectangles of cardboard larger than twelve by eighteen inches.

In determining the shape of the poster it is well to remember that the square is less interesting than the rectangle; also that one of the most pleasingly proportional rectangular shapes has its dimensions in the ratio of one to one and a half, as suggested in the dimensions mentioned in the preceding paragraph.

On the opposite page is a sample poster.

DIRECT MAIL

A short mimeographed form letter concerning the play can be issued at but slight expense. It is not practicable for every community, but quite effective in many. Such letters should be signed by the publicity manager or the director. There are usually younger brothers of the cast who will eagerly undertake the house to house distribution of such letters for a small sum of pocket money.

THE PAID ADVERTISEMENT

And, lastly, there is the paid display advertisement in the newspaper. In cities the cost of such an advertisement will likely be prohibitive. But in small commu-

THE TERRIBLE MEEK

A RELIGIOUS DRAMA BY
CHARLES RANN KENNEDY
GIVEN BY SPECIAL PERMISSION OF
HARPER AND BROS. OF NEW YORK

THE PARK BOULEVARD

PRESBYTERIAN CHURCH

SUNDAY, APRIL 6, 8 P.M.

FIGURE 5
AN EFFECTIVE POSTER

nities such an advertisement justifies itself. The same principles apply to the paid display advertisement as apply to the poster.

PUTTING OUT PUBLICITY ON TIME

The amateur publicity man usually makes the mistake of delaying his publicity until a few days before the production. News stories should begin to *reach the papers two weeks before the production* and should be followed up with a fresh story every day or two thereafter. More than one insertion of a paid advertisement is seldom justified. In the small community with a weekly paper this insertion should be made in the issue of the week preceding the production. If the community boasts a daily paper and the play is to be given on a Sunday evening, the Saturday issue of the paper is the logical one in which to place the advertisement. Material for the printed church bulletins should be in the pastor's hands well in advance of the set day of the week upon which he sends his notes to the printer. Posters should be in place ten days to two weeks before the production. The direct mail letters are sometimes used to best advantage as a last-minute reminder of the play to bring it freshly back to memory on the very eve of its performance. But even when so used there is a proper time for their preparation and delivery. Timeliness is absolutely vital to effective publicity.

Chapter XIII

EQUIPMENT

GOOD dramatic equipment need not necessarily be expensive but its possession is essential. Modern audiences, even in the small country villages, are accustomed to seeing their plays, especially their movies, well set, well costumed, and well lighted. The church drama group cannot hope to win respect if its productions are crudely staged.

THE STAGE

The first thing to remember in the planning of the stage is the fact that the rectangular opening through which the audience views the play—the proscenium arch —is very like a picture frame. The size of that frame must be in due proportion to the human figures which are seen through it. This rectangular opening should be *not less than twenty feet wide and twelve feet high.*

Second, the living picture framed by the arch of the proscenium must be so placed as to be seen to the best advantage. An ideal height for the stage floor is *three feet nine inches above the floor* of the auditorium itself.

Third, that portion of the stage not seen by the audience is just as important to the success of the play as the visible area. There must be room "off-stage" for the handling of scenery, the manipulation of lighting effects and the presence of actors awaiting their entrances or those who must pass from one side of the stage to the other behind the scenes. *There should be as much room on either side and behind as is contained in the playing space itself.* Moreover, the space above the stage —the flies—is important. Low stage ceilings are a continual nuisance. The ceiling of the stage should be at least two feet higher than the top of the proscenium arch so as to allow for the hanging of border lights and fly curtains above the playing space. In a good theatre the flies extend above the stage to such a height as will allow pieces of scenery such as interior walls and sky drops to be drawn upward out of sight on pulley lines and fastened there overhead until needed. This is not only a convenient way of handling these pieces but it also saves valuable off-stage space.

Suitable dimensions for the smallest stage which should ever be built may be given as: *twenty-four feet wide, eighteen feet deep, twelve feet high, elevated three feet nine inches above the floor level. Groups with less space than this will be annoyingly cramped.*

Proportions for a medium sized stage are: forty-two feet wide, twenty-one feet deep, with a proscenium opening twenty-eight feet wide and twenty-one feet high.

Proportions for a large stage are: fifty-six feet wide, twenty-eight feet deep, with a proscenium opening thirty-five feet wide and twenty-eight feet high.

This proportioning of the proscenium rests upon the rule that the height of the proscenium arch should be seven feet less than its width for the most pleasing architectural effect. In actual play production, of course, the full height of such arches as given for the medium and large stages are never used. The extra height is masked off by the "tormentor" curtain which hangs down just inside the proscenium and may be raised or lowered to

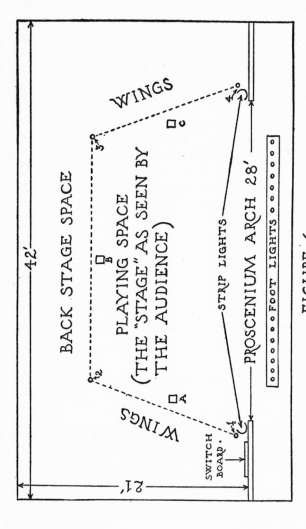

FIGURE 6

FLOOR PLAN OF MEDIUM SIZED STAGE

give the overhead space most pleasing to the particular stage set being used.

For a more detailed idea of these proportions and an explanation of the terms used in speaking of the various parts of the stage, Figures 6 and 7 should be consulted.

The stage floor should always be of soft wood in order that the stage screws used in making fast those pieces of scenery which need bracing may bite into the wood easily.

DRESSING ROOMS AND TOILET FACILITIES

It is important that provision be made for dressing rooms and toilet facilities for both sexes along passageways adjoining the stage proper. There must be at least one dressing room for men and one for women. Each dressing room will, of course, be furnished with a shelf or table for the players' use as a dressing stand. There will be drawers for make-up material, and mirrors and lights so adjusted that the player's face will receive the same amount and kind of light that it receives upon the stage. Each room should, if possible, be supplied with hot and cold running water.

THE COSTUME CLOSET

Every efficient dramatic organization will early find its need for a costume closet. This should be a room fitted with racks and hangers where garments worn in one play may be safely encased in moth and dust proof bags and hung away for future need. The costume closet will also have a set of large and small drawers, each labeled, where smaller articles of costume and unfash-

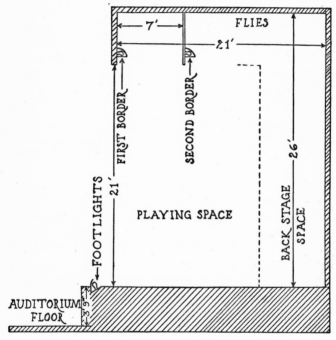

FLIES

7'

21'

FIRST BORDER

SECOND BORDER

26'

21'

FOOTLIGHTS

PLAYING SPACE

BACK STAGE SPACE

AUDITORIUM FLOOR

3'9"

FIGURE 7
SECTION THROUGH MEDIUM SIZED STAGE

ioned fabrics used in draping may be stored. There should further be shelves to hold such costume accessories as shoes, sandals, and hats.

There should also be set aside a closet, or at least a large cupboard, where small properties such as the pottery jars and staffs of biblical plays and the pistols, desk telephones, electric bells and what-not of modern ones can be safely locked away. This closet may be used also for storing the easily lost or broken odds and ends of the lighting equipment such as bulbs, colored gelatines and fuses.

The lighting units needed, together with their general description, wiring, and location upon the stage have already been discussed in the chapter upon LIGHTING. Although the scientifically designed equipment placed upon the market by commercial manufacturers is generally superior to that which the members of the drama group can contrive for themselves, it is yet possible to make satisfactory lighting apparatus at low cost. Let the group with limited funds take courage.

Strips and borders may be simply contrived by screwing porcelain electric light sockets in a continuous row down one side of a strip of two-by-three spruce or pine of the length desired. These should be wired in parallel according to the color series to be used in the bulbs and the wiring carried down the back of the strip. A strip of polished tin of sufficient width to bend into a reflecting trough is then prepared by cutting out a series of holes down its center line which will allow it to fit down over the light sockets. With such a reflector rounded into the proper shape and fastened to the wooden strip the electric bulbs may then be screwed in and the whole is ready for use. Bolted upright to a portable wooden standard such a trough of lights may be used as a strip light from the wings. Suspended overhead it makes an acceptable border light.

Flood lights may be contrived by running an electric socket capable of feeding a two hundred watt lamp through the bottom of a deep tin dish pan or a large tin pail and making the whole fast to a wooden support. Color screens for such flood lights can be fashioned by framing sheets of colored gelatine in light wooden frames between the sides of which runs a coarse supporting mesh of fine wires. Gelatines can be purchased from any dealer in stage lighting equipment.

Rheostats for dimming the lights may be made by fastening round disks of Bakelite or other insulating material over the tops of half gallon Mason fruit jars. In each disk two holes should be bored through which small metal rods of copper or aluminum provided with non-conducting handles can be lowered into the jar. The positive wire of the lighting circuit is fastened to the top of one of these rods, the negative to the top of the other. One rod is left in the jar, the other out. The jar itself is filled with water in which a handful of salt has been dissolved. When the second rod is lowered into the jar a dim glow of light will appear in the bulbs upon the circuit as the rod first touches the solution. When it is fully immersed the lights will be at their full intensity. Only experimentation can determine the amount of salt to be dissolved in the water. The stronger the solution the better conductor of current the water becomes and the sooner the lights will brighten after the second rod touches the water. The aim should be to have the lights reach full intensity only after the second rod is fully immersed. Such a rheostat will care for a two hundred watt flood very nicely. For heavier loads a larger container than the half gallon jar must be used though the same principle may be applied.

Spot lights must be purchased.

A unified switch board for the entire stage lighting may be constructed by installing a series of push-plug sockets on a large board. All of these sockets will be separately wired into one common lead-in cable heavy enough to carry the load for the entire stage lighting which will in turn require a special connection for the lead cable itself. Each socket will be controlled by a knife switch upon the board and its wiring should be supplied with its own fuse. All electric cables leading to the separate lighting units should be fitted with push plug connections so that they can be plugged into this switch board at the will of the operator. A sufficient number of the sockets on the board should have rheostat connections to allow the operator and his assistants to dim any or all the lighting units as needed.

Such home-made lighting equipment is a bit crude, and the switchboard especially is far from ideal, yet it works, and it is inexpensive. With patience some very fine lighting effects can be had from it. In constructing it care should be taken throughout to check upon the requirements of fire insurance policies and local ordinances.

SETTINGS

The two most generally useful settings for the church stage are the draped background and that formed by fabric-covered flipper screens.

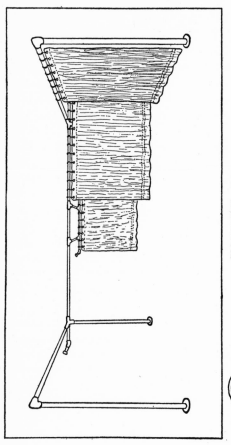

FIGURE 8

IRON-PIPE FRAME FOR HANGING DRAPES. AT
LEFT A DETAIL SHOWING HOW DRAPE IS
FASTENED TO FRAME BY SPECIAL CURTAIN
PIN ENCIRCLING PIPE AND HOOKING THRO'
GROMMET IN CANVAS WEBBING.

The draped background may be either semi-circular or rectangular. In either case the drapes are best finished off at the top by sewing a strip of canvas webbing on the back side. Holes may then be punched and brass grommets inserted. The drapes are hung from an iron-pipe frame work by means of special safety pins such as are used for shower bath curtains (see Figure 8). These pins encircle the pipe and then hook through the grommets. The iron-pipe frame work is supported by standards of the same piping which may be set in sockets in the stage floor (see 1, 2, 3, and 4, Figure 6). Such sockets are sunk flush with the floor and may be covered by flat screw lids when the drapes are not in use, thus making the drapes ideal for temporary use in the chancel as well as upon the parish house stage. The lower hems of all draperies should be weighted by sewing in lengths of iron chain. This serves to prevent undue swaying of the draperies when hung.

Entrances are formed by gaps left in the curtains. If the rectangular shape of a room is carried out, the supporting pipe at the rear should extend well out beyond the side walls and carry sufficient additional drapery to mask entrances left at upper left and right. An opening left in the rear wall may be masked by a backing strip of the drapery hung from an extra frame of the piping.

Window and door frames may be set against such drapes, but *it is better to avoid this so far as possible*. A supposed window may be represented by locating it well downstage where it will be concealed from the actual view of the audience by the intervening folds of drapery masking the side of the stage behind the proscenium. There it may be vividly suggested by a stream of incoming light from a flood with an amber color screen located in the wings.

In constructing all rectangular sets it is desirable to distort the general shape by pulling in the sides of the room slightly as they approach the rear wall. This will enable persons seated even well to the side of the auditorium to see the full sweep of the rear wall.

A draped stage will serve very acceptably if done in a neutral gray, a dull blue, or a forest green, all of which can be considerably altered in hue by the play of colored lighting. For great flexibility in color effects one may make the hangings of a neutral shade of rep cloth on which has been sprayed red, green, and aluminum paints in mingled effect. Each color of light in the border and strips will then pick out its own counterpart in the drapery and tend to minimize its complement. Thus by dimming out any two colors in the lighting the drapery will at once assume the richness of the remaining color of light, while when under the play of all the lights it will form a background of neutral gray.

Flipper screens, or wings, are simply tall, two-section screens hinged so as to fold either way. They are constructed by tacking drapery material in large folds over light but firmly constructed wooden frames. Three by nine feet is a satisfactory set of dimensions for the framework of a single section of one of these double screens. The ones used with such good effect in the Riverside Church in New York are four by twelve feet.

Such screens are set up, open-book fashion, so as to support themselves in the upright position. They require no bracing so may be set up easily and quickly for use in the chancel as well as upon the parish house stage. Moreover, with such small units forming the walls, the shape of the set can be varied greatly. Still further, by covering various faces of these screens with various fabrics in various colors in eight or ten inch folds, the possibilities for the construction of interesting stage sets from their various combinations become almost limitless. Suggestions for the construction of such screens, together with many illustrations of their use, can be found in *Worship Through Drama* by Alexander and Goslin, Harper's, 1930. A simple drawing is shown in Figure 9.

Next in importance is the cyclorama. The cyclorama is a smooth, white, semi-circular surface in the form of a section of a cylinder placed in the rear of the acting area as far back upon the stage as will still leave an acceptable passageway behind it. When played upon by colored lights it creates an illusion of atmospheric depth. This cyclorama is often constructed of white canvas stretched smoothly over a support of iron piping. When not in use it is rolled up on a vertical roller at one side of the stage. If within the means of the group, a far more efficient background of this type is found in the plaster dome which stands in the same position upon the stage but curves high up and over the playing space as well as in beyond its sides. Lacking the means for the construction of either the plaster dome or the cyclorama, a fair substitute may be found in a plain white canvas back drop, or in a flipper screen.

An almost infinite number of suggestive and beautiful settings may be arranged by constructing a set of archways together with tall, three-section screens which may be set up to represent square pillars. These archways and pillars combined with different steps and platform levels, draperies, and the use of the cyclorama for dis-

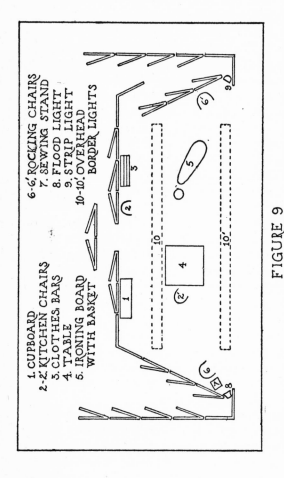

1. CUPBOARD
2-2' KITCHEN CHAIRS
3. CLOTHES BARS
4. TABLE
5. IRONING BOARD
   WITH BASKET

6-6' ROCKING CHAIRS
7. SEWING STAND
8. FLOOD LIGHT
9. STRIP LIGHT
10-10' OVERHEAD
      BORDER LIGHTS

FIGURE 9

MODIFIED SET FOR THE NEIGHBORS. FLIPPER SCREENS ON
OPEN PLATFORM. REAR WINDOW MOVED DOWNSTAGE
AND SUGGESTED BY LIGHT FROM A FLOOD.

tant atmospheric vistas give a flexible set which can be adapted for almost any conceivable scene.

Last of all, and *least in value*, one may construct a set of flats for arranging interior settings. These flats are made of canvas stretched over wooden frames and then painted or papered in suitable interior designs. They are made in uniformly sized sections which can be lashed together from the rear by a peg and cord device, and they are made rigid upon the stage by the use of stage braces screwed to the floor. With several extra flats on hand, including door and window sections as well as plain, the shape and ordering of an interior may be greatly varied from time to time.

THE CURTAIN

The best curtain for amateur use is of the draw type. Steel rings should be sewn upon the back side and at a little distance below the top so that a "heading" is formed above them which will hide the supporting rod and draw cords. The curtain is hung upon a length of iron pipe by means of the rings and is drawn open and shut by cords threaded through the rings and running to one side of the stage over small pulley blocks. More lasting satisfaction, however, will be gained by an additional investment in a curtain track for carrying the curtain, dispensing with the rings and cords. Such a track can be bought from a theatrical supply house and is easily installed.

The most beautiful material for the curtain is a heavy, thick piled velvet, but this is very expensive. The curtain may well be made of the same material as that with which the stage is draped. If the material used is not heavy or thickly woven, however, it will need to be lined to make it light proof. For a semi-transparent curtain not only annoys an audience by allowing light to filter through, but destroys the illusion and mood of the play by only half-concealing the movements of the stage hands.

DRAPERY MATERIALS

A general list of materials useful for stage draperies is here given together with their usual widths as they come from the bolt. Prices vary so from year to year that it is impossible to give any estimate of costs.

Velvet, 39 inches wide

Velour, 54 inches wide

Washable corduroy, 36 inches wide

Monk's cloth, 50 inches wide

Rep cloth, 49 inches wide

Colored art denim, 36 inches wide

Decorative burlap, 35 inches wide

Canvas for the construction of a cyclorama may be had in 72-inch widths.

Chapter XIV

THE ENVELOPING SERVICE OF WORSHIP

HERE is an example of an enveloping service of worship for a religious drama:

A DRAMATIC SERVICE OF WORSHIP FOR EASTER EVE

Organ Prelude, *Passion Chorale*—Hans L. Hassler, arr. by Bach

Invocation:

> Blessed Lord, who for our sakes wast content to bear sorrow and want and death, grant unto us such a measure of thy Spirit that we may follow thee in all self-denial and tenderness of soul. Help us by thy great love to succour the afflicted, to relieve the needy and destitute, to share the burdens of the heavy laden, and ever to see thee in all who are poor and desolate. Amen.

—BISHOP WESTCOTT

Hymn, *O God, Our Help in Ages Past*—Isaac Watts; Tune: *St. Anne*

> O God, our help in ages past,
> Our hope for years to come,
> Our shelter from the stormy blast,
> And our eternal home!
>
> Under the shadow of thy throne
> Still may we dwell secure;
> Sufficient is thine arm alone,
> And our defense is sure.

Before the hills in order stood,
    Or earth received her frame,
From everlasting thou art God,
    To endless years the same.

A thousand ages, in thy sight,
    Are like an evening gone;
Short as the watch that ends the night,
    Before the rising sun.

The busy tribes of flesh and blood,
    With all their cares and fears,
Are carried downward by the flood,
    And lost in following years.

Time, like an ever-rolling stream,
    Bears all its sons away;
They fly forgotten, as a dream
    Dies at the opening day.

O God, our help in ages past,
    Our hope for years to come;
Be thou our guide while life shall last,
    And our eternal home!

Scripture:

    If ye keep my commandments, ye shall abide in my love; even as I have kept my Father's commandments, and abide in his love.

    These things have I spoken unto you, that my joy might remain in you, and that your joy might be full. This is my commandment, that ye love one another, as I have loved you. Greater love hath no man than this, that a man lay down his life for his friends.

                     —JOHN 15: 10–13

    And when they were come to the place which is called Calvary, there they crucified him, and the malefactors, one on the right hand, and the other on the left.

.   .   .   .

And one of the malefactors which were hanged railed on him, saying, "If thou be Christ, save thyself and us." But the other answering rebuked him, saying, "Dost not thou fear God, seeing thou art in the same condemnation? And we indeed justly; for we receive the due reward of our deeds: but this man hath done nothing amiss." And he said unto Jesus, "Lord, remember me when thou comest into thy kingdom." And Jesus said unto him, "Verily I say unto thee, today shalt thou be with me in paradise."

—LUKE 23: 33, 39–49

Prayer:

O God, Immortal and Invisible, forgive the faltering faith of those whose dwelling is among the mortal and the seen. We have no sight for unseen things, and we may have missed Thee at every turn. Every common bush may flame with fire, but we have no time to turn aside, and our hardened feet do not apprehend the holy ground. The heavens may declare Thy glory, but our eyes are too earthbound to read their story of infinity and peace. Day unto day may utter speech, but our ears are deaf with inward strife, and we hearken not nor understand. We have brooded long on the pain and anguish of the world, but we can read no redemption in the cross to which humanity is nailed; we have looked into the faces of our fellows, but discern no divine impression there; we have found little to love in the brother whom we have seen, how can we hope to love the God whom we have not seen? And now the awful fear has crept upon us that we are blind.

O Lord, that we might receive our sight. Amen.

—W. E. ORCHARD, *The Temple, A Book of Prayer*

Hymn, *Come, O Thou Traveler Unknown*—Charles Wesley; Tune: *St. Catherine*

> Come, O thou Traveler unknown,
>   Whom still I hold, but cannot see;
> My company before is gone,
>   And I am left alone with thee:
> With thee all night I mean to stay,
> And wrestle till the break of day.
>
> I need not tell thee who I am,
>   My sin and misery declare;
> Thyself hast called me by thy name,
>   Look on thy hands, and read it there:
> But who, I ask thee, who art thou?
> Tell me thy name, and tell me now.
>
> 'Tis Love! 'Tis Love! thou diedst for me!
>   I hear thy whisper in my heart;
> The morning breaks, the shadows flee;
>   Pure, universal love thou art:
> To me, to all, thy mercies move;
> Thy nature and thy name is Love.
>
> I know thee, Saviour, who thou art,
>   Jesus, the feeble sinner's Friend;
> Nor wilt thou with the night depart,
>   But stay and love me to the end:
> Thy mercies never shall remove;
> Thy nature and thy name is Love.

A Religious Drama, *The Two Thieves*—Esther Willard Bates
  (This play tells in simple but powerful fashion how the two thieves who were crucified with Jesus meet in a lonely, wind-swept region of darkness between the

worlds. The one is blinded by his own unbelief and is filled with bitterness because of his suffering. Both are lost and terrified. In ministering to the need of his brother the first thief wins a vision of Jesus and the light of heaven falls down upon his seeing eyes. But even with the entrancing vision of paradise before his eyes the first thief refuses to desert the need of his blind and despairing brother. The wonder of this refusal begins to take possession of the second thief. For the first time he realizes the full depth of human love. In a moment of self-renunciation he urges the first thief to leave him and go on to Paradise. And in that moment his eyes too are opened. Through love and self-sacrifice he has been redeemed. The heavenly light deepens to a radiant path along which the two thieves, hand in hand, make their way beyond the sight of the audience while the distant songs of the angels rise higher and higher welcoming the two to the presence of God.)

Offertory, *Chorale: Ich ruf' zu Dir, Herr Jesu Christ*—Bach

Hymn, *O Master, Let Me Walk With Thee*—Washington Gladden; Tune: *Canonbury*

> O Master, let me walk with thee
> In lowly paths of service free;
> Tell me thy secret; help me bear
> The strain of toil, the fret of care.
>
> Help me the slow of heart to move
> By some clear, winning word of love;
> Teach me the wayward feet to stay,
> And guide them in the homeward way.
>
> Teach me thy patience; still with thee
> In closer, dearer company,
> In work that keeps faith sweet and strong,
> In trust that triumphs over wrong.

In hope that sends a shining ray
Far down the future's broadening way;
In peace that only thou canst give,
With thee, O Master, let me live.

Benediction:

Now unto him that is able to do exceedingly abun-
dantly above all that we ask or think, according to the
power that worketh in us, unto him be glory in the
church by Christ Jesus throughout all ages, world
without end. Amen.

—Ephesians 3: 20, 21

In such a service of worship as that just given the
drama and the worship supplement and strengthen each
other. The opening portion of the service should prepare the congregation intellectually and emotionally to
receive the message of the play. The play in turn,
through the very intensity of its emotional revelation
of the divine in human life should turn the hearts of
the worshipers with renewed praise and consecration
back to God. This result is the ideal to be sought in the
presentation of any religious drama.

The consummation of such an ideal, however, cannot come without careful preparation. This preparation
should begin among the players and the congregation.
True worship is impossible in a congregation which has
come together to be amused or among players who work
guided by the idea of putting on an entertainment or of
seeking applause. Let the players work together from
the very first with the thought of making their play an
instrument of public worship. And let the congregation
be carefully led to approach the entire service in the
same attitude. Let all announcements of the play carry
out this idea of worship, not of entertainment.

Nor can a spirit of worship ensue from a haphazard mingling of passages of Scripture, extemporaneous prayers, and the jazz strains of cheap gospel songs. It can come only through carefully planning the entire service beforehand in the light of the message of the play and under the guidance of intelligence, good taste, and sincere religious purpose. The person responsible for planning such a service of worship will proceed, in general, through the following steps:

DETERMINING THE WORSHIP THEME

First the play will be studied to determine its mood and its message. Next, the person building the worship service will set down the theme of the play in writing, stating it in a single, positively worded, clear-cut, declarative sentence. Thus the theme of Charles Rann Kennedy's *The Terrible Meek* is this: The meek shall inherit the earth. The theme of Esther Willard Bates' *The Two Thieves* is: He that loses his life for the love of Christ shall find it. And the theme of Mary P. Hamlin's *He Came Seeing* is: He who loves father or mother more than Jesus is not worthy of him. Around the theme he will then build every item of the worship service so as to develop it, enrich its meaning, and bring it at last to climactic expression in the play itself.

SELECTING THE SCRIPTURE

Next the Scripture reading will be chosen. Sometimes, where a biblical play is to be given, the Scripture will be chosen to give a background for the play. More often the Scripture will be chosen to give expression to the theme of the play or to enrich its meaning. In all events the Scripture should be chosen out of a feeling for its special fitness rather than mechanically by running down the key word of the theme in a concordance of the Bible.

THE PRAYERS

The prayer of general petition should not be left to the inspiration of the moment, nor should the invocation and the benediction be determined by mere customary use. Every prayer used should be written or selected or at least seriously pondered with the idea of giving the maximum of spiritual power for the particular service at hand. The Scripture abounds in beautiful and appropriate passages for invocations and benedictions based upon many themes. Moreover, the Church has a vast store of devotional literature garnered through the centuries of her' life. There is no reason why the leader of a worship service should always feel bound to depend upon prayers of his own composition. Let the treasure house be opened to enrich the lives of the congregation! The printed programs will give proper credit to the source. In all the prayers let the builder of the service strive for simplicity, sincerity, appropriateness, vigor, and beauty. And let him avoid too great length as well as any complexity of thought.

SELECTING THE MUSIC

In selecting hymns the first thing to look for is appropriateness of thought in the light of the worship theme. The words of the hymns chosen need not state the theme directly but they must contribute definitely to its development or enrichment or give a background against which it will stand out with added strength.

Moreover, they must be sincere, vital instruments for the worship of Eternal God, not mere sentimental expressions of human emotion. As poetry they must be more than crudely contrived rhymes. They should abound in beauty and stimulate the imagination. Yet at the same time they must avoid that which is merely flowery or extravagant. Such hymns there are in abundance in the rich treasury of the church, although, unfortunately, our modern era has produced but few.

Next, these appropriate words must be wed to a worthy and appropriate tune—a tune which not only bears out the thought and mood of the verse but is in itself a fit musical expression for the worship of God. Both the unmitigated jazz of *Brighten the Corner Where You Are* and the sickly sentimentality of *In the Garden* must be left far behind when the true worship of God is the aim. Dr. Davison puts the whole matter clearly when he writes:

Ideal religious music should so act upon the hearer as to wring from him the cry, "How good and how great is the *Lord God,*" rather than that he should say, "How good this music makes *me* feel." [1]

As a guide in the selection of worthy tunes the builder of the worship service will remember the following points:

Every hymn tune is the product of three factors: melody, rhythm, and setting. These should all be appropriate one to the other.

The melody must be preeminently singable. Its range should not exceed an octave and a third and it should be written in such a key that the highest note will never

[1] Davison, Archibald T.: *Protestant Church Music in America,* p. 36.

exceed E flat. There should be no difficult intervals, consecutive skips in the same direction, or jumpy passages. The melody should have a smooth and graceful melodic flow. Examples of good melodies are: *Dundee, Old Hundred, Dominus Regit Me, Ein' Feste Burg, Crusader's Hymn.*

The rhythm should be interesting but simple. There should be a sufficient amount of repetition of rhythmical pattern to ensure unity in the whole. Moreover, the rhythm needs to fit the thoughts and words of the hymn. Rhythms which march or which suggest the dance are not conducive to the spirit of worship.

The setting needs to be appropriate to the melody. A few hymns have contrapuntal settings (one part singing against the other), but most are harmonic (consisting of a series of chords). The melody, carried by the soprano, is most important. The bass is of next importance. It should be strong and have an interesting movement. The inner parts also need vitality. A harmonic setting should be simple (*Dundee* is a fine example), but not dull and crude as is usually the case with gospel songs. Pompous settings should be avoided (*Ancient of Days*). The frequent use of incidental sharps or flats sentimentalize a tune (*Serenity*).

The majority of our best hymn tunes date from Protestant composers of the sixteenth, seventeenth, and eighteenth centuries. The nineteenth century is characterized by the growth of sentimentality although it has given us a few excellent tunes such as *Hamburg, Regent Square,* and *Canonbury.* The old plainsong of the early church forms the source of much religious music of high worth, as do also the religious folk songs. *Hamburg* is an adaptation of an early plainsong and *Crusader's Hymn* is based upon a German folk song.

ORDERING THE SERVICE

In ordering the dramatic service of worship the play should come as the climax. If it is a good play it is capable of bearing its own message without being preceded or followed by sermonic comment. Drama has a vividness to which few sermons can attain. When the play comes to an end on its own emotional peak, the theme has been given its most forceful expression. Let there then be a moment's pause of meditation, a brief prayer, an offering, a closing hymn, and then the benediction. Above all, let there be no applause of the play. Let there be a note on the printed programs, or a word from the leader to this effect. A religious drama is given for its religious values, not for the glory of its actors.

THAT MATTER OF THE OFFERING

Let the offering be an act of worship. Experience has shown that it comes best after the play where it forms an outlet for the emotional surge of the congregation. It is a valid and definite way in which the people can feel that they are contributing their substance in the same spirit in which the players contributed their time and talent.

A SELECTED LIST OF RELIGIOUS DRAMAS

THE plays that follow have been selected from more than a thousand read and subjected to the tests of religious drama noted on pages 24–27 of this manual. The selection has been for the use of adults and older young people rather than for children.

These plays are classified as to subject matter and season on pages 183–185.

A. COLLECTIONS

Dramatic Preludes and Services of Worship, by ISABEL KIMBALL WHITING. Nine services—one for each month from October to June inclusive—each a prelude dramatizing from the Bible or Christian history some spiritual exploration in the search for "God as companion." Baker. $1.50.

Free Company Presents, The, compiled by JAMES BOYD. A collection of ten radio plays by well-known dramatists, as originally presented on the air by the Columbia Broadcasting System. Most of them adaptable for one-act play production. Dodd, Mead and Company. $2.00.

Little Plays of St. Francis, by LAURENCE HOUSMAN. Complete edition (45 plays) in three volumes. (Contents of each upon request.) Each volume sold separately, price, $2.00. Some of the plays (lists supplied) are available in separate acting editions. Price, each, 50 cents. Acting time, each, about 30 minutes. Speaking parts average six to eight, mostly Brothers of the Franciscan Order. In a few plays there are speaking parts for women. The living character of St. Francis of Assisi in a cycle of plays from legendary sources and from the records of history. (Royalty, single plays, $5.00. Special arrangements where more than one play is used.) Book prices given above. Baker.

Modern Religious Dramas, compiled by FRED EASTMAN. Nine one-act plays and a pageant, all modern in setting and religious in effect. Includes: *Neighbors*, by ZONA GALE; *Confessional*, by PERCIVAL

WILDE; *What Men Live By*, by VIRGINIA CHURCH; *The Valiant*, by HALL and MIDDLEMASS; *Bread*, by FRED EASTMAN; *The Deathless World*, by J. M. S. TOMPKINS; *El Cristo*, by MARGARET LARKIN; *Dust of the Road*, by KENNETH SAWYER GOODMAN; *The Color Line*, by IRENE TAYLOR MacNair; *The Christmas Pageant of the Holy Grail*, by W. RUSSELL BOWIE. Harper's. $1.00.

Plays of American Life, by FRED EASTMAN. One three-act and seven one-act plays, each centering around a modern social and spiritual conflict in American life. Includes *The Tinker*, *The Great Choice*, *Bread*, *Our Lean Years*, *The Doctor Decides*, *The Ragged Edge*, *Courtship*. French. $1.50.

Plays for Seven Players, by CHARLES RANN KENNEDY. Eight plays by the author of *The Servant in the House*. University of Chicago Press. $5.00.

Plays to Live By, compiled by HAROLD EHRENSPERGER. Five one-act plays by various authors. Abingdon–Cokesbury. 25 cents.

Sinner Beloved and Other Modern Biblical, Miracle, and Morality Plays, The, by PHILLIPS E. OSGOOD. Two of these are designed for the parish house, seven for the church. Harper's. $2.00.

Ten One-Act Plays, compiled and edited by FRED EASTMAN. Themes of social significance: war and peace, loyalty, beauty amid squalor, nationalism versus religion, Christmas in the modern world. The volume includes: *Monsignor's Hour*, by EMMET LAVERY; *Pawns*, by PERCIVAL WILDE; *Prize Money*, by LOUIS WILSON; *The Great Choice*, by FRED EASTMAN; *He Came Seeing*, by MARY P. HAMLIN; *Tidings of Joy*, by ELIZABETH McFADDEN; *The Tail of the Dragon*, by ELLIOT FIELD; *The Lord's Prayer*, by FRANÇOIS COPPÉE; *Twentieth Century Lullaby*, by CEDRIC MOUNT; *Peace I Give Unto You*, by DOROTHY CLARKE WILSON. Willett, Clark. $2.00.

Thirteen by Corwin. Radio dramas by NORMAN CORWIN. Although not designed as religious dramas, two or three of these are religious in effect. All exemplify the power and the technique of radio drama. Holt. $2.75.

Three One-Act Plays, by MARY KATHARINE REELY. Realistic, daily-life plays, centering around home, labor, and love. Baker. $1.00.

Twelve Months of Drama, by DOROTHY CLARKE WILSON. Twelve one-act plays—some biblical, some modern—each with a suggested worship service. Baker. $1.75.

B. INDIVIDUAL PLAYS

Adeste Fidelis, by LOUISE AYRES GARNETT. A Christmas processional in blank verse. Music selected and arranged by MACK EVANS.

Fifteen men, twelve women, and choir. Thirty minutes. 35 cents. (Royalty, $5.00.) Baker.

America on Trial, by FRED EASTMAN. A pageant-play in one act, dealing imaginatively with America's present crisis. No scenery. Thirty to forty characters. 35 cents. (Royalty, $5.00.) French.

And He Came to His Father, by ERNA KRUCKMEYER. One act. Scene: an exterior. Costumes: Biblical. Plays forty minutes. Four men, two women, and extras. 35 cents. (No royalty.) French.

At the Junction, by RACHEL FIELD. Story of a girl violinist who loses her courage on the eve of a concert—and then finds it again. Two men, one woman, one girl of eleven. 35 cents. (Royalty, $5.00.) French.

Ba Thane, by EDNA A. BALDWIN. A one-act play of Burma. Four men, three women. 25 cents. (No royalty.) Student Volunteer Movement.

Bishop's Candlesticks, The, by NORMAN MCKINNEL. One act. Three men, two women. A dramatized incident from Victor Hugo's *Les Misérables*. 30 cents. (Royalty, $5.00.) French.

Bread, by FRED EASTMAN. One act. Two men, three women. About twenty-five minutes. The struggle of a modern family for economic independence and culture. (See also the sequel, *Our Lean Years*.) 30 cents. (Royalty, $5.00.) French.

But Mother—, by MARIE REGIER. One act. Three men, three women. About thirty minutes. Humorous but poignant struggle between first and second generations in a German Mennonite family. 35 cents. (Royalty, $5.00.) French.

Child of the Frontier, A, by ELMA E. LEVINGER. A story around the birth of Abraham Lincoln. One act. Three women. 50 cents. (No royalty.) Appleton–Century.

Christmas Destiny, by DOROTHY C. ALLAN. A poignant story of a young bank clerk about to run away from the consequences of his wrong-doing, but saved by the Christmas spirit of an older and wiser man. A brief poetic prologue and epilogue in the mood of fantasy. Three men, four women. 35 cents. (No royalty.) Baker.

Christmas, Incorporated, by WALTER KERR. A one-act play for women. A department-store clerk, disillusioned by the commercialization of Christmas, is shown by a little child where Christmas may really be found. Six women, one child. 35 cents. (Royalty, $5.00.) French.

Christmas Pageant of the Holy Grail, The, by W. RUSSELL BOWIE. Four scenes, arranged for reader and tableaux. Twelve to fifteen characters. King Arthur and his Knights, the Round Table, and the Holy Grail, in pageant form. 25 cents. (No royalty.) Abingdon–Cokesbury.

Color Line, The, by IRENE TAYLOR MacNAIR. One act. Three men, three women. About thirty minutes. The problem of the missionary in China and the Chinese student in America. 15 cents. (No royalty.) Missionary Education Movement.

Come Let Us Adore Him, by VICTOR STARBUCK. A poetic play of the Nativity. Three scenes. Twelve men, five women, and one child. 50 cents. (Royalty, $10.00 when admission is charged; $5.00 otherwise.) Dramatic Publishing Co.

Coming of Christ, The, by JOHN MASEFIELD. Designed for the chancel. Thirteen men, one woman, several attendants, and a chorus. A poetic production of great beauty, but difficult. $1.75. (Royalty on application.) Music separate, by GUSTAV HOLST. 90 cents. Baker.

Crowded Out, by J. W. G. WARD. One act with prologue and epilogue. The traditional Christmas story done simply and effectively and with use of the Christmas carols. Twelve men, six women. 25 cents. (Royalty, $5.00.) Harper's.

Curtain, The, by HALLIE FLANAGAN. One act. Four men, two women. Theme: The importance of the habit of personal honesty. Prize play of the Des Moines Little Theater. 35 cents. (Royalty, $5.00.) French.

Devil and Daniel Webster, The, by STEPHEN VINCENT BENÉT. A one-act fantasy dramatizing Benét's famous story. Eleven men, one woman, and extras. 35 cents. (Royalty, $5.00.) Dramatists Play Service.

Doctor Decides, The, by FRED EASTMAN. A modern one-act play centering about a medical missionary in the southern mountains whose financial support fails. Three men, three women. 35 cents. (Royalty, $5.00.) French.

Dust of the Road, by KENNETH SAWYER GOODMAN. A one-act drama. Three men and one woman. A dramatization of the old legend that Judas is allowed to return to earth once a year to plead with some soul tempted to betray friendship. 50 cents. (Royalty, $5.00 if no admission is charged; $10.00 if admission is charged.) Baker.

Early American, by MARION WEFER. Prize-winning peace play of the 1938 contest sponsored by the Religious Drama Council of the Greater New York Federation of Churches. Three men, three women, and extras. 30 cents. (No royalty.) French.

El Cristo, by MARGARET LARKIN. One act. Four men, two women. About twenty-five minutes. The crucifixion of the spirit versus the crucifixion of the body. A story of the Penitentes in New Mexico. 50 cents. (Royalty, $10.00.) French.

Eternal Life, by FRED EASTMAN. One act. Two men, three women, and a boy (or girl). A new and timely dramatic incident in a family air-raid shelter. Makes use of Christmas carols or Lenten hymns. 35 cents. (Royalty, $5.00.) French.

Far Country, The, by DOROTHY CLARKE WILSON. A short one-act play of the story of Abraham presented as a drama of youth and the great adventure. Three men, two women. 35 cents. (No royalty.) Baker.

Finger of God, The, by PERCIVAL WILDE. Two men, one girl. The struggle of a man with his conscience. 35 cents. (Royalty, $5.00.) Baker.

Gillean, by CUMMING KENNEDY. A full-length play in three acts and an epilogue, all in free verse. Eight men, two women, and extras. One setting. A story of the courage and nobility of unpretending Scots farmers in a northern prairie state. Rare combination of poetry, drama, and religion. Requires skilled direction and acting. 75 cents. (Royalty, $25.00.) French.

Great Choice, The, by FRED EASTMAN. A peace play in one act, dramatizing the conflict of great loyalties: Religion vs. Nationalism. Four men, four women. 35 cents. (Royalty, $5.00.) French.

Haven of the Spirit, by MERRILL DENISON. A one-act play on the theme of religious freedom. An episode in the life of Roger Williams. Thirteen men, one woman, and extras. 30 cents. (No royalty.) Dramatists Play Service.

He Came Seeing, by MARY P. HAMLIN. One act. One setting, simple interior of a house in Jerusalem. Three men, two women, and neighbors, including a few children. A dramatization of the story of loyalty to a great cause. 35 cents. (Royalty, $5.00 when no admission is charged; $10.00 when admission is charged.) French.

Joint Owners in Spain, by ALICE BROWN. One act. Four women. 35 cents. (Royalty, $5.00.) Baker.

King Shall Reign, A, by MARION WEFER. One act. Two men, four women. A mother, whose child has been a victim of Herod's slaughter of the innocents, bitterly nurses her sorrow until Joseph and Mary visit her briefly on their flight into Egypt. 35 cents. (Royalty, $5.00.) French.

Least of These, The, by VIRGINIA W. ELICKER. A dramatization for a speaking chorus. A modern interpretation of the Lord's Prayer and of certain sayings of Jesus applied to present social conflicts. Requires at least twelve, male or female. 50 cents. (No royalty.) Baker.

Let Every Heart—, by MARY KATHARINE REELY. A modern one-act, twenty-minute play telling the story of how Christmas comes to patients, nurses and visitor in the corner of a hospital ward. Five women. 30 cents. (Royalty, $5.00.) Dramatic Publishing Company.

Long Christmas Dinner, The, by THORNTON WILDER. A one-act play dramatizing the brevity of life. Five men, seven women. Five other plays in the volume with this title. $2.50. (Royalty, $10.00.) French.

Lord's Prayer, The, by FRANÇOIS COPPÉE. One act. Three women, three men, and two extras (soldiers). A story of the French commune. 35 cents. (Royalty, $3.00.) Baker.

Lost Children, by DOROTHY E. NICHOLS. A Christmas play for children, in one act. Six girls, three boys. 50 cents. (Royalty, $10.00 where admission is charged; $5.00 where no admission is charged.) Longmans, Green and Co.

Lowly King, The, by MARTHA BAYLY SHANNON. One act. Three men, two women, and a chorus of off-stage voices. An imaginary episode in the home of a Jewish family—friends of Jesus—just before his triumphal entry into Jerusalem. 35 cents. (License for first performance given with purchase of five copies. Additional performances, $1.50 each.) Baker.

Nativity, The, by ROSAMOND KIMBALL. Four scenes. Nine young men, two women, children. A Christmas service arranged for a reader from biblical text, and tableaux. 35 cents. (No royalty.) French.

Neighbors, The, by ZONA GALE. One act. Two men, six women. Humorous treatment of a dramatic situation in a village. Religious in its effect on an audience. About one hour. 50 cents. (Royalty, $10.00 when admission is charged; $5.00 when it is not.) French and Baker.

One Night in Bethlehem: A Play of the Nativity, by KATHERINE S. BROWN and GLENNA SMITH TINNIN. In a prologue and five scenes. Twenty men, six women, and carolers. 35 cents. (Royalty, $5.00 where no admission is charged; $10.00 where admission is charged.) French.

Our Lady's Tumbler, by RICHARD SULLIVAN. One act. Three men, one woman. A dramatized version of the medieval French legend of a tumbler who became a monk and offered his tumbling as a sacrificial gift to the statue of the Virgin. 35 cents. (Royalty, $5.00.) Dramatic Publishing Company.

Our Lean Years, by FRED EASTMAN. A one-act play in which a practical, co-operative, religious effort saves a home threatened with financial disaster. Same characters as in *Bread*. Eight men, six women. 35 cents. (Royalty, $5.00.) French.

Outward Bound, by V. SUTTON VANE. Three acts. Six men, three women. One interior. Modern costumes. The scene is laid on board a ship outward bound, but whither? It is gradually learned that all the characters, with two exceptions, are dead. The play is religious in effect. $1.75. (Royalty on application to the publisher.) French.

Pageant of Worship, A, by a class in pageant construction at The Chicago Theological Seminary. A pageant setting forth in dramatic form the place of the Bible, the Cross, and the Lord's Supper in Christian worship. Designed for reader and pantomime. No scenery. Seven characters, reader, and choir. 35 cents. (No royalty.) Baker.

Pawns, by PERCIVAL WILDE. One act. Six men characters. Characters are simple peasants on either side of the Austrian-Russian frontier. Having been friends for generations, war makes them enemies and brings disaster until they reassert their common humanity. 35 cents. (Royalty, $10.00.) Baker.

Peace I Give Unto You, by DOROTHY CLARKE WILSON. A peace play especially suitable for Christmas. One act. Four men, one woman. 35 cents. (No royalty.) Baker.

Prize Money, by LOUIS WILSON. One-act play of the struggle for beauty as well as bread on a farm. Two men, three women. 35 cents. (Royalty, $5.00.) Baker.

Resurrection, The, by ROSAMOND KIMBALL. Four scenes. Twelve men, three women, the voice of Jesus. An Easter service arranged for tableaux and a reader from biblical text. 35 cents. (No royalty.) French.

Return of the Prodigal, The, by ELMA EHRLICH LEVINGER. One act. Simple scene. Five men, one woman, neighbors. 50 cents. (No royalty.) Pilgrim Press.

Rock, The, by MARY P. HAMLIN. Three acts, four scenes. Six men, five women. A character study of Simon Peter. 50 cents. (Royalty, $10.00 when admission is charged; $5.00 otherwise.) French.

Saint, The, by A. BEATRICE KNOWLES. A story about the original St. Nicholas and Christmas giving. One act. One man, nineteen boys, fourteen girls. 35 cents. (Royalty, $5.00.) French.

Saint's Return, The, by ESTHER WILLARD BATES. A fantasy in one act. Six men, four women. A group of saints in convocation in the Half-Way House to Heaven despair of improving this warring world. The arrival of an old man and his daughter, victims of the war but still lovers of humanity, puts new heart in the saints. 35 cents. (Royalty, $5.00 when admission is charged; otherwise free.) Baker.

Salute to the Fourth, A, by ELIZABETH MCFADDEN. A one-act play dramatizing the spirit of the Bill of Rights. Six men, one woman, and extras. 30 cents. (No royalty.) Dramatists Play Service.

Ship Forever Sailing, by STANLEY YOUNG. A dramatization of the signing of the Mayflower Compact. Thirteen men, two women, and extras. 30 cents. (No royalty.) Dramatists Play Service.

Slave with Two Faces, The, by MARY CAROLYN DAVIES. An allegory in one act. Four men, three women. 35 cents. (Royalty, $5.00.) French.

Spreading the News, by LADY GREGORY. One act. Seven men, three women. About forty minutes. A delightful satire of gossipy neighbors. 50 cents. (Royalty, $5.00.) French.

Summoning of the Nations, The, by ELISABETH WOODBRIDGE MORRIS. A pageant in verse interpreting the contribution and spirit which each nation has made toward the beauty and knowledge of the present world. Thirty-one characters, men or women, and chorus. 35 cents. (No royalty.) French.

Summons of Sariel, The, by MAGDALENE KESSIE. A fantasy in one act, for nine women, or three men and six women. A college girl who has met with an auto accident finds herself in "the timeless interval between Time and Eternity" awaiting, with others, the summons of the Angel of Death. Will she live or die—and how? 35 cents. (Royalty, $5.00.) Dramatic Publishing Company.

Sunrise, by LOUIS WILSON. A one-act peace play of biblical times. Four men, one woman. 35 cents. (Royalty, $3.00.) Baker.

Tail of the Dragon, The, by ELLIOT FIELD. A one-act missionary play of China. Three men, two women. 15 cents. (No royalty.) Missionary Education Movement.

Tardy April, by LOUIS WILSON. One-act comedy of women's missionary society in a rural community. One man, four women. 35 cents. (No royalty.) Baker.

Tenant Farmers, by ELLIOT FIELD. One act. Three men, one woman, and a girl. The family of a "Dust Bowl" farmer (not a tenant) struggles to maintain their courage and integrity in the face of great hardship and social injustice. 35 cents. (No royalty.) Baker.

Terrible Meek, The, by CHARLES RANN KENNEDY. A tense story of a soldier's struggle with his conscience after the crucifixion of Jesus. Mary plays an important part. One act. Two men, one woman. To be played in darkness. 35 cents. (No royalty.) Baker.

Thy Son Liveth, by MARYANN E. MANLY. One act. Three men, one woman, one boy. Simple interior. A quietly powerful play about the rich young ruler and Zacchaeus and the choice which both faced. Especially suitable for Easter and the Lenten season. 35 cents. (Royalty, $5.00.) Baker.

Tidings of Joy, by ELIZABETH McFADDEN. A modern Christmas play about a young American couple faced with eviction on Christmas Eve and befriended by a group of carol singers, scouts, and others animated by the Christmas spirit. Six men, two women, four boys, four girls, and other children. 35 cents. (Royalty, $10.00 with admission; $5.00 otherwise.) French.

Tinker, The, by FRED EASTMAN. A three-act humorous modern comedy of spiritual power, religious in its effect. Plays two hours.

Four men, three women. One set, a living-room. 75 cents. (Royalty, $15.00.) Baker.

Traveling Man, The, by LADY GREGORY. A one-act miracle play for Christmas. One man, one woman, one boy. 50 cents. (Royalty, $5.00.) French.

Tree of Paradise, The, by ESTHER WILLARD BATES. A humorous Christmas fantasy about an old German who goes to Paradise and complains at what he finds there. Fifteen characters, men or women. 35 cents. (Royalty, $5.00 where no admission is charged; $10.00 where admission is charged.) Baker.

Trouble with the Christmas Presents, The, by MARY P. HAMLIN. A comedy in prologue and one act. Four boys, five or six girls. 35 cents. (Royalty, $5.00.) French.

Triumph of the Defeated, The, by FRED EASTMAN. An Easter pageant. Eight speaking parts; thirteen non-speaking parts; an organist, and invisible choir. No scenery. Designed for the chancel or church platform. Plays about one hour. The theme is the ultimate triumph of the courageous and righteous souls who are defeated by the forces of fear and hatred. 35 cents. (Royalty, $5.00.) French.

Two Thieves, The, by ESTHER WILLARD BATES. One act. Two men, a choir (unseen), a harpist (unseen). A short dialogue play for Good Friday. 35 cents. (Royalty, $5.00.) Baker.

Valiant, The, by HOLWORTHY HALL and ROBERT MIDDLEMASS. One act. Five men, one woman. A story of a sacrifice made by a criminal to keep a knowledge of his shame from his family. 50 cents. (Royalty, $10.00.) Longmans, Green and Co.

We Call It Freedom, by DOROTHY CLARKE WILSON. A timely one-act play on the theme of race relations. Four women, including one taking the part of an intelligent and cultured Negro maid. 25 cents. (No royalty.) Missionary Education Movement.

What Men Live By, a dramatization by VIRGINIA CHURCH of the story of LEO TOLSTOI. One act, two scenes. Five men, three women, two children. 35 cents. (Royalty, $10.00.) Baker.

Why the Chimes Rang, by ELIZABETH McFADDEN. One act. One man, one woman, two children, extras. Chorus and chimes needed. 35 cents. (Royalty, $5.00 where no admission is charged; $10.00 otherwise.) French.

World Without End, by ALBERT JOHNSON. A poetic, choric drama. Through interpretive dance, choric speech, and dramatic episodes the actors set forth the conflict and triumph of Christ's way of life. Time: two hours. Highly skilled direction needed. 50 cents. (Royalty on application.) Baker.

C. Manuals

Art of Play Production, The, by JOHN DOLMAN, JR. Harper's, 1928. 466 pp. $2.75.

Bible Dramatics, by J. W. RAINE. D. Appleton–Century Co., 1927. 372 pp. $2.00.

Church Play and Its Production, The, by ESTHER WILLARD BATES. A new manual covering not only the usual subjects of directing, acting, costuming, lighting, etc., but writing and the special adaptations of all the dramatic arts for the production of plays in the church chancel. Illustrated. Baker, 1938. 303 pp. $2.75.

Costuming the Biblical Play, by LUCY BARTON. Illustrated by DAVID SARVIS. Condensed, but thorough. Baker. $1.35.

Craftsmanship of the One-Act Play, The, by PERCIVAL WILDE. A standard work on the technique of play writing, with special reference to the one-act play. Little, Brown. $3.00.

Creative Dramatics, by WINIFRED WARD. For the upper grades and high schools. D. Appleton–Century Co., 1930. 304 pp. $2.25.

Drama in the Church, by FRED EASTMAN and LOUIS WILSON. Sums up briefly the most important things drama groups should know for the task of producing plays in churches, not as entertainment, but as a means of ministering to the souls of men through a great art. French. $1.50.

Dramatic Calendar for Churches, A, by HAROLD A. EHRENSPERGER. Suggestions for dramatic programs for outstanding events in each month. International Council of Religious Education. 25 cents.

Fundamentals of Play Directing, by ALEXANDER DEAN. A practical handbook and guide for the amateur or professional director by the late associate professor of play directing at Yale. Farrar and Rinehart. $4.00.

General Principles of Play Direction, by GILMORE BROWN and ALICE GARWOOD. A practical guide book by the director of the Pasadena Community Playhouse and his assistant. French. $2.50.

Home-Built Lighting Equipment for the Small Stage, by THEODORE FUCHS. Gives specific instructions supplemented by drawings. French. $2.50.

How's Your Second Act? by ARTHUR HOPKINS. French, 1931. 43 pp. $1.00.

Lighting the Stage with Homemade Equipment, by J. S. KNAPP. Illustrated. Baker, 1933. $1.25.

Living Drama, The, by NELLIE MILLER. D. Appleton–Century Co., 1924. 437 pp. $2.50.

New Theatres for Old, by MORDECAI GORELIK. Unique and stirring account of the rise and fall of stage and screen techniques. French. $4.50.

Ventures in Dramatics, by HULDA NIEBUHR. A manual designed especially for teachers of boys and girls ten to fifteen years old. Actual record of the educational process and the resulting playlets worked out by such groups in the Madison Avenue Presbyterian Church, New York. Scribner's, 1935. 223 pp. $1.75.

Writing the One Act Play, by HAROLD N. HILLEBRAND. A concise and clearly written manual for the beginner. Crofts. $1.75.

CLASSIFICATION OF PLAYS

*

LENTEN AND EASTER

Dust of the Road
  (Can easily be adapted for Easter by the changing of one or two lines)
El Cristo
Eternal Life
Gillean
He Came Seeing
King Shall Reign, A
Lord's Prayer, The
Lowly King, The
Pageant of Worship, The
Resurrection, The
Rock, The
Saint's Return, The
Summons of Sariel, The
Terrible Meek, The
Thy Son Liveth
Triumph of the Defeated, The
Two Thieves, The
What Men Live By
World without End

CHRISTMAS

Adeste Fidelis
Christmas Destiny
Christmas, Incorporated
Christmas Pageant of the Holy Grail, The
Come Let Us Adore Him
Coming of Christ, The
Crowded Out
Dust of the Road
Eternal Life
Let Every Heart—
Long Christmas Dinner, The
Lost Children
Nativity, The
One Night in Bethlehem
Peace I Give Unto You
Saint, The
Saint's Return, The
Tidings of Joy
Tinker, The
Traveling Man, The
Tree of Paradise, The
Trouble with the Christmas Presents, The
Why the Chimes Rang

BIBLICAL

And He Came to His Father
Far Country, The
He Came Seeing
King Shall Reign, A
Lowly King, The
Return of the Prodigal
Rock, The

Sinner Beloved, A
Sunrise
Terrible Meek, The
Thy Son Liveth

Tardy April
We Call It Freedom

PEACE

Early American
Great Choice, The
Pawns
Peace I Give Unto You
Summoning of the Nations, The
Sunrise
Terrible Meek, The

SOCIAL AND INDUSTRIAL

America on Trial
Bread
Doctor Decides, The
Least of These, The
Our Lean Years
Prize Money
Tenant Farmers
Tidings of Joy
We Call It Freedom

PATRIOTIC

America on Trial
Child of the Frontier, A
Devil and Daniel Webster, The
Early American
Haven of the Spirit
Pilgrim Mother, A
Salute to the Fourth, A
Ship Forever Sailing

MISSIONS

Ba Thane
Color Line, The
Doctor Decides, The
Tail of the Dragon, The

GENERAL

America on Trial
At the Junction
Bishop's Candlesticks, The
Bread
But Mother—
Child of the Frontier, A
Curtain, The
Devil and Daniel Webster, The
Doctor Decides, The
Dust of the Road
El Cristo
Far Country, The
Finger of God, The
Gillean
Great Choice, The
Haven of the Spirit
Joint Owners in Spain
Least of These, The
Lord's Prayer, The
Neighbors
Our Lady's Tumbler
Our Lean Years
Outward Bound
Pageant of Worship, A
Pawns
Pilgrim Mother, A
Prize Money
Return of the Prodigal
Saint's Return, The
Slave with Two Faces, The
Spreading the News
Summoning of the Nations, The
Tardy April
Terrible Meek, The
Tinker, The
Valiant, The
We Call It Freedom
What Men Live By
World without End

*

NON-ROYALTY PLAYS

And He Came to His Father
Ba Thane
Child of the Frontier, A
Christmas Destiny
Christmas Pageant of the Holy
    Grail, The
Color Line, The
Early American
Far Country, The
Haven of the Spirit
Least of These, The
Nativity, The
Pageant of Worship, A

Peace I Give Unto You
Resurrection, The
Return of the Prodigal
Salute to the Fourth, A
Ship Forever Sailing
Sinner Beloved, A
Summoning of the Nations, The
Tail of the Dragon, The
Tardy April
Tenant Farmers
Terrible Meek, The
We Call It Freedom

A SELECTED LIST OF
LONGER PLAYS OF SPIRITUAL POWER

Recommended for reading, but too difficult for most amateur groups to produce. Groups considering them for production should write the publishers for royalty requirements.

Abe Lincoln in Illinois. By ROBERT E. SHERWOOD. Dramatists Play Service. $2.00.
Bethlehem. By LAURENCE HOUSMAN. Baker. 50 cents.
Brothers Karamazov. By DOSTOEVSKY. Doubleday, Doran. $1.00.
Bury the Dead. By IRWIN SHAW. Random House. $1.00.
Caponsacchi. By ARTHUR GOODRICH and ROSE PALMER. Dramatists Play Service. $1.00.
Corn Is Green, The. By EMLYN WILLIAMS. Random House. $2.00.
Cyrano de Bergerac. By EDMUND ROSTAND. Baker. 75 cents.
Dark Hours, The. By DON MARQUIS. Doubleday, Doran. $1.75.
Days Without End. By EUGENE O'NEILL. Random House. $2.50.
Dear Brutus. By J. M. BARRIE. Scribner's. $1.00.
Death Takes a Holiday. By WALTER FERRIS. French. 75 cents.
Devil Passes, The. By BENN W. LEVY. French. $2.00.
End of Summer. By S. N. BEHRMAN. Dramatists Play Service. 75 cents.

Excursion. By VICTOR WOLFSON. Dramatists Play Service. 75 cents.

Family Portrait, The. By LENORE COFFEE and WILLIAM J. COWEN. French. $2.00.

Field God, The, and *In Abraham's Bosom.* By PAUL GREEN. Both in one volume. French. $2.00.

Goose Hangs High, The. By LEWIS BEACH. French. 75 cents.

Green Pastures, The. By MARC CONNELLY. Dramatists Play Service. $1.00.

Hell Bent for Heaven. By HATCHER HUGHES. French. 75 cents.

Here Come the Clowns. By PHILIP BARRY. French. $2.00.

John. By PHILIP BARRY. French. $2.00.

Johnny Johnson. By PAUL GREEN. French. $2.00.

Little Foxes, The. By LILLIAN HELLMAN. Dramatists Play Service. 75 cents.

Loyalties. By JOHN GALSWORTHY. Scribner's. $1.00.

Men in White. By SIDNEY KINGSLEY. Covici Friede. $2.00.

Minick. By EDNA FERBER and GEORGE S. KAUFMAN. French. 75 cents.

Murder in the Cathedral. By T. S. ELIOT. French. $1.25.

Our Town. By THORNTON WILDER. French. 75 cents.

Outward Bound. By V. SUTTON VANE. French. $1.75.

Passing of the Third Floor Back. By JEROME K. JEROME. French. 75 cents.

Peace on Earth. By SKLAR and MOLTZ. French. 75 cents.

Prexy and Son. By FRED EASTMAN. Baker. 75 cents.

R.U.R. By KAREL CAPEK. French. 75 cents.

Saint Joan. By GEORGE BERNARD SHAW. Dodd, Mead and Co. $2.50.

Shadow and Substance. By PAUL VINCENT CARROLL. Dramatists Play Service. 75 cents.

Silver Cord, The. By SIDNEY HOWARD. French. 75 cents.

Susan and God. By RACHEL CROTHERS. Dramatists Play Service. 75 cents.

Ten Greek Plays. By AESCHYLUS, SOPHOCLES, and EURIPIDES. Translated by GILBERT MURRAY and others. Oxford. $3.50.

Tinker, The. By FRED EASTMAN. Baker. 75 cents.

Trial of Jesus, The. By JOHN MASEFIELD. Macmillan. $1.75.

Valley Forge. By MAXWELL ANDERSON. French. 75 cents.

Wednesday's Child, and *House We Live In.* Both in the same volume. By LEOPOLD ATLAS. French. $2.00.

Winterset. By MAXWELL ANDERSON. Dramatists Play Service. 75 cents.

Yellow Jack. By SIDNEY HOWARD. Dramatists Play Service. 75 cents.

Yellow Jacket, The. By GEORGE C. HAZLETON and BENRIMO. French. 75 cents.

You and I. By PHILIP BARRY. French. 75 cents.

PUBLISHERS

Abingdon–Cokesbury Press, 150 Fifth Ave., New York, N. Y. 810
  Broadway, Nashville, Tenn.
D. Appleton–Century Co., 35 West 32d St., New York, N. Y.
Walter H. Baker Co., 178 Tremont St., Boston, Mass.
Covici Friede, Inc., 432 Fourth Ave., New York, N. Y.
Dodd, Mead and Company, Inc., 443 Fourth Ave., New York, N. Y.
Doubleday, Doran, Garden City, Long Island, N. Y.
Dramatic Publishing Co., 59 East Van Buren St., Chicago, Ill.
Dramatists Play Service, 6 East 39th St., New York, N. Y.
Farrar and Rinehart, 232 Madison Ave., New York, N. Y.
Samuel French, Inc., 25 West 45th St., New York, N. Y. 811 West
  7th St., Los Angeles, Calif.
Harcourt, Brace & Co., 383 Madison Ave., New York, N. Y.
Harper and Brothers, 49 East 33d St., New York, N. Y.
Houghton Mifflin Co., 2 Park St., Boston, Mass.
Longmans, Green and Co., 55 Fifth Ave., New York, N. Y.
Macmillan Company, 60 Fifth Ave., New York, N. Y.
Missionary Education Movement, 150 Fifth Ave., New York, N. Y.
Oxford Press, 114 Fifth Ave., New York, N. Y.
Pilgrim Press, 14 Beacon St., Boston, Mass.
Random House, 20 East 57th St., New York, N. Y.
Charles Scribner's Sons, 597 Fifth Ave., New York, N. Y.
Student Volunteer Movement, 156 Fifth Ave., New York, N. Y.
University of Chicago Press, 58th St. and Ellis Ave., Chicago, Ill.
Willett, Clark and Co., 407 South Dearborn St., Chicago, Ill.